Elementary BASIC
with Applications

Elementary BASIC with Applications

Mario V. Farina

Telecommunications & Information Processing Operations
General Electric Company

PRENTICE-HALL, INC., Englewood Cliffs, New Jersey

To
ERNIE DENBY

Current printing (last digit):
10 9 8 7 6 5 4 3 2 1

(P) 13-252916-5
(C) 13-252924-6

Library of Congress Catalog Card Number: 74-135239
Printed in the United States of America

Prentice-Hall International, Inc., London
Prentice-Hall of Australia, Pty. Ltd., Sydney
Prentice-Hall of Canada, Ltd., Toronto
Prentice-Hall of India Private Limited, New Delhi
Prentice-Hall of Japan, Inc., Tokyo

Preface

This book is intended for:

1. Persons who wish to learn the techniques of programming a computer.

2. Persons who have just finished a formal course in a programming language such as FORTRAN, COBOL, PL/I, ALGOL or BASIC and are having difficulty learning how to attack real-life problems.

When learning how to program, one finds that there is a good deal more to it than simply learning a language. A person may be an expert in the mechanics of some language but, given a problem to solve, doesn't know how to *begin*. In this book we explore some of the techniques programmers use when they solve problems. Not all techniques are shown since no single book could possibly hold them all, but many of the more important ones are included. Often, the techniques described are given in simplified form. In my opinion, it is better that a beginner thoroughly understand a useful, though simplified, technique than not understand a far more sophisticated one.

This book serves two purposes. It teaches the major features of BASIC, the time-sharing programming language but, more important, it shows how a computer can be programmed. The knowledge gained in learning to apply BASIC can be easily transferred to whatever other language one is using.

Since learning techniques and their applications is more important than learning a language, I chose a language which is exceedingly easy to master, BASIC. (It almost teaches itself.) This language was developed under the direction of Professors John G. Kemeny and Thomas E. Kurtz at Dartmouth College under the terms of a grant by the National Science Foundation. In many business firms, schools, government agencies, and in the armed forces, remote terminals are available whereby persons may access distant computers using BASIC.

If you are fortunate enough to have a terminal near you, practice what you learn in this book. Try all the examples and work out the exercises. You'll make rapid and, hopefully, enjoyable progress. If you have no terminal available, your progress may be slower, but it will be steady since the text progresses step-by-step from the simplest of problems to those which are much more complex. Only enough of the BASIC language has been presented to enable learning the techniques and applications in this book. Persons who wish to obtain a more complete understanding of BASIC may obtain my book on the subject, *Programming in BASIC, The Time-Sharing Language,* Prentice-Hall, Inc., 1968.

In this book, many problems are presented from the fields of science and business. The scientific problems are rather simple and require only a knowledge of Algebra and Trigonometry. Answers are given to all problems in the back. The student should study the solutions until he understands them completely. In some cases, he may have to write flowcharts from the solutions so that the techniques used become more clear.

A comprehensive index is also provided in the back of the book.

Books never write themselves. Many persons combined their efforts to create this text. I am indebted to scores of people including these: Dante J. Pellei, Miss Nancy D. George, Joseph Tocco, Nelson Rosenstein, Joseph L. Katz and R.J. Hawke.

A careful job of proofreading and program-testing was done by Claude J. DeRossi and Mrs. Beatrice Shaffer. Mrs. Shaffer also typed the text.

Mario V. Farina

Contents

Chapter 1

WHAT IS TELETYPE TIME-SHARING ?

Imagine a large computer at a central location, say down-
town New York, operated by an organization which offers a
computing service. You may avail yourself of this service by
sitting at a remote terminal, typically a teletype, picking
up a phone attached to the terminal, and dialing the computer.

When the computer responds, you type instructions to the
computer, then obtain answers at once. If, while you are
typing your instructions, you make a mistake, the computer
will tell you and give you a chance to make corrections.

Computer users, like yourself, are at remote points from
one another. You are not even aware of the fact that others
are using the computer at the same time as you. The reason
for this illustion is that the computer is fast and *shares
time*. This means that user A will be serviced, then user B,
user C, etc. Each user gets a brief portion of the computer's
attention. For example, User A may receive only one second
of actual computer time; User B may get two seconds. The
amount of computer time that an individual gets is based, to
a large extent, upon what he wants the computer to do.

If User A has a lengthy job requiring say ten to fifteen
seconds of actual computer time, the computer will first give
him a couple of seconds, then service other users, then come
back to him and pick up from where it left off.

A computer is fast; it can make thousands of calculations *per second*. Therefore, it has little difficulty in servicing 40, 50 or even as many as 200 users simultaneously. Very rarely will a user be forced to wait for answers, and even then for only a few seconds.

People *subscribe* to computer service in much the same way as they subscribe for telephone or electric service. When you subscribe, you'll be given a *user number* which identifies you.

Let's say Joe Brown is an engineer who wants to solve a mathematical problem quickly. He turns to his teletype presses a button marked ORIG, then dials the computer's phone number.

The computer types a message announcing its readiness to serve. The computer types:
USER NUMBER--
Joe types his user number. Here's what the teletype paper looks like at that time (the example user number is ficticious):
USER NUMBER--X99999
The computer will then want to know what programming language Joe intends to use. Several languages may be available. In this text we'll use BASIC because its easiest to learn and use.

The computer's message and Joe's reply look like this:
SYSTEM--BASIC
Now, the computer will want to know whether Joe intends to write a new program or use one he wrote and saved another day. Assume he intends to write a new one. The conversation continues like this:
NEW OR OLD--NEW

2

The computer will request a name for the new program. That name may have up to 6 characters:

NEW FILE NAME--EQ3

The computer types READY.

Now Joe may begin typing instructions to the computer using the BASIC programming language. The instructions constitute a *program*. When Joe has finished typing his program he types RUN. The computer will then type answers.

Here's an example of a complete conversation that Joe may have with the remote computer:

GE TIME-SHARING SERVICE
ON AT 9:48 03 WED 12/16/70 TTY 6
USER NUMBER--X99999
SYSTEM--BASIC
NEW OR OLD--NEW
NEW FILE NAME--EQ3
READY.
10 PRINT 3.20 + 6.70 + 8.30
20 PRINT (3.4 * 9.6) - 7.1
RUN

EQ3 9:50   03 WED 12/16/70

 18.2
 25.54

USED 1.50 UNITS
BYE
*** OFF AT 9:50 ELAPSED TERMINAL TIME = 1 MIN.

The messages typed by the computer are underlined. Joe has typed everything else.

The illustrations you see in this book have all been worked out on GE's time-sharing service, Mark I. The time-sharing service you subscribe to may be provided by another concern. It is inevitable,therefore, that you'll notice differences between what we show you in this book and what you actually encounter. The differences should be minor and cause you very little, if any, inconvenience.

Here is the keyboard of one of the teletypes you may be working with. It's for the widely-used model 33 unit. Your machine may well be another unit. If so, some of the keys and buttons we mention may be somewhat different. If you have any problems, your sales representative will be very happy to answer them.

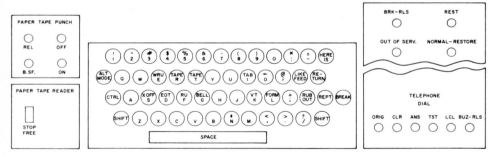

Figure 1-1

There are many problems in this book to solve. If you have access to time-sharing, be sure to actually try out the examples and work out the exercises. When you've written a program you would like to save, type the word SAVE whenever the system types READY, or when it pauses waiting for a command from you.

Whenever you wish to unsave a program, bring it into memory by typing OLD when the system types READY. The system will ask the name of the program, then make it available to you. Type the word UNSAVE and it will disappear from your catalog area.

To find out which programs are saved in your catalog area, type the word CAT or CATALOG.

****

BASIC MINI-LESSON:

Several chapters in this book will be followed by mini-lessons which summarize the BASIC language features presented in the chapter. In this chapter you learned that when conversing with the computer you may use these words: BASIC, NEW, OLD, PRINT, BYE, RUN, SAVE, UNSAVE, CAT, CATALOG.

In addition you will be asked to give your user number and, from time to time, names for new programs.

Chapter 2

CALCULATIONS

Often, your problem will be to solve some rather complicated equations. You can use a desk calculator or a slide
rule, of course, but a computer is faster and more accurate.
In this chapter, we'll show how to give the computer equations involving additions, subtractions, multiplications,
divisions, exponentiations, square roots, sines, cosines,
and logs.

Let's begin with some simple problems. Suppose you
want to perform this calculation:

$$3.20 + 6.70 + 8.30 = ?$$

where the numbers represent costs for a new device being de-
signed.

Sit down at your teletype machine, call up the computer
and type this:

```
10 PRINT 3.20 + 6.70 + 8.30
RUN
```

Some BASIC systems may require you to place an END statement at the end of each program. If your computer tells you
that you have forgotten the END statement, include statement
99999 END in all your programs. The above program would look
like this:

```
10 PRINT 3.20 + 6.70 + 8.30
99999 END
RUN
```

The computer will sum 3.20, 6.70, and 8.30, then type
out the answer on the teletype's paper like this:

```
EX2-1        13:55      03 WED 12/16/70

  18.2
```

What about that number "10" which appears ahead of the
word PRINT? That's a *line number*. Most instructions you
give the computer will require line numbers. We'll have more
to say about such numbers soon.

You'll note that the word RUN does not require a line number. It tells the computer to execute the previous instructions. RUN is called a *system command*. You'll be introduced
to other system commands as we go along.

Spacing is not important when you write BASIC statements.
In general, you may place blanks wherever you please. Place
at least one blank following line numbers.

Let's try another calculation:

$$3.26 + 7.61 + 8.45 + 7.20 = ?$$

(Say these are your entertainment expenses for four weeks in
July.)

What you type and what the computer responds is this:

```
10 PRINT 3.26 + 7.61 + 8.45 + 7.20
RUN
```

26.52

Now let's try a more difficult problem. Suppose you have these two calculations to make:

$$\frac{4.7}{-8.3} + 3.7 = ?$$

and

$$(3.4 \times 9.6) - 7.1 = ?$$

Your instructions to the computer and its reply look like this:

```
10 PRINT (4.7/-8.3) + 3.7
20 PRINT (3.4*9.6) - 7.1
RUN
```

EX2-3   13:57   03 WED 12/16/70

3.13373
25.54

The two statements at lines 10 and 20 are executed in the order that they appear. Note that the answers are not labelled. We'll discuss labelling soon. You don't have too much control over how many decimal places you receive in your answers. BASIC has standard output formats but usually you'll find that this causes no great problems. You've now learned that + means *add*, - means *subtract*, * means *multiply* and / means *divide*.

8

Each of the statements above except for RUN has a line number. Line numbers may be any number from 0 thru 99999. They must be in increasing sequence. You may leave gaps between numbers. It's OK to begin with line 10, and then number the next line 25. You'll see later why you should leave gaps between line numbers.

Note the parentheses. The only parentheses available are (and). As you can see, parentheses are used to make sure the computer understands exactly what is to be calculated. Don't hesitate to insert parentheses where you believe they *may* be needed. Too many parentheses will not hurt your program at all. Too few will give you wrong answers. Consider this calculation, for example:

$$\frac{3.2 + 6.4}{4.7} = ?$$

Would you write your instructions like this?

```
10 PRINT 3.2 + 6.4/4.7
RUN
```

Certainly not! It appears that you want the computer to calculate

$$3.2 + \frac{6.4}{4.7} = ?$$

Here's the correct way to write the BASIC instruction for

$$\frac{3.2 + 6.4}{4.7} = ?$$

```
10 PRINT (3.2 + 6.4)/4.7
RUN
```

or

```
10 PRINT (3.2 + 6.4)/(4.7)
RUN
```

In the latter example, the parentheses around 4.7 are not necessary, but they don't hurt.

The rule about parentheses is: *If in doubt, put them in.*

Now you're ready to try some more elaborate calculations:

$$\frac{\dfrac{-4.8}{7.6} \times \dfrac{2.7}{-8.3} + 7}{5.4 \times 8.3} = ?$$

This is easily written in BASIC like this:

```
10 PRINT (((-4.8/7.6)*(2.7/-8.3))+7)/(5.4*8.3)
RUN
```

It's OK to place parentheses *within* parentheses. *The computer deals with innermost parentheses first,* then works its way toward outer parentheses.

The computer responds with:

```
EX2-4          14:01      03 WED 12/16/70

.160764
```

Study the placement of the parentheses. Not all of them are essential, but you can see that the parentheses we've used make the calculations to be done completely clear.

Now we're ready to try calculations which involve square roots, logs, and trigonometric functions.

Here's one to practice with:

$$\sqrt{7.4} - 8.3 = ?$$

In BASIC you write:

```
10 PRINT SQR(7.4) - 8.3
RUN
```

The computer responds with:

```
EX2-5    14:01    03 WED 12/16/70
-5.57971
```

Observe how you obtain the square root of 7.4. You write SQR and place in parentheses the number for which you want the square root. SQR is a *function* and the number you place in parentheses is the function's *argument*. (An argument is the value that a function needs in order to work.)

Try this problem:

$$\sin .23 - \sqrt{\cos (3.4 + \sqrt{3})} = ?$$

You've probably already guessed that SIN and COS are functions available in BASIC. You type this:

```
10 PRINT SIN(.23) - SQR(COS (3.4 + SQR (3)))
```

and the computer responds:

```
EX2-6    14:03    03 WED 12/16/70
-.410342
```

11

Just a few comments about the calculation shown above. SIN and COS are BASIC functions requiring *radian* arguments. Note also that all arguments must *be in parentheses*. It's not all right to type:

10 PRINT SIN .23 - SQR(COS(3.4 + SQR(3)))

The radian value .23 must be enclosed within parentheses.

You'll note, too, that it's OK to have functions within functions. Above, the argument for the square root is

$$cos\ (3.4 + \sqrt{3})$$

In turn, the argument for the cosine function is $3.4 + \sqrt{3}$.

The fact that you must enclose all arguments within parentheses explains the many parentheses shown in the BASIC statement.

Functions available in BASIC are:

NAME	USE
SIN(X)	Compute sine of X
COS(X)	Compute cosine of X
TAN(X)	Compute tangent of X
ATN(X)	Find arctangent of X
EXP(X)	Compute e^X
ABS(X)	Find absolute value of X
LOG(X)	Find natural logarithm of X
SQR(X)	Take square root of X
RND(X)	Obtain a random number
INT(X)	Extract largest integer of X

We'll discuss all these functions as we go along.

You'll often have to raise values to various powers. Suppose you have this problem:

$$\sqrt{3.5^3} + \ln 3^{4 \cdot 2} = ?$$

In BASIC you'd write instructions like these:

```
10 PRINT SQR (3.5↑3) + LOG (3↑4.2)
RUN
```

Note that in BASIC, LOG means *natural* log.

The computer responds:

```
EX2-7        14:04        03 WED 12/16/70

11.1621
```

The up-pointing arrow permits you to raise a value to any power you require. Be sure that what you ask for is mathematically reasonable. For example, you can't raise a negative value to a power such as 2.5. In mathematics -8 raised to the 2.5 power has no meaning.) You can, however, raise a negative value to an integer power such as 5. (In mathematics -8 raised to the 5th power is -32768.)

Let's try this problem:

$$\left[\sqrt{\frac{3.6}{2.7^5}} + \frac{\sin .2}{\log_e 1.3} \right]^3 = ?$$

This is written in BASIC as:

```
10 PRINT (SQR((3.6/2.7↑5) + (SIN(.2)/LOG(1.3))))↑3
RUN
```

13

The computer responds:

    EX2-8   14:31   03 WED 12/16/70
        .691948

Where parentheses don't otherwise indicate, the computer's hierarchy of operation is:

First, all exponentiations are computed.

Second, all multiplications and/or divisions in any order, scanning the expression from left to right, are computed.

Third, all additions and/or subtractions in any order, scanning the expression from left to right, are computed.

The business student may have noticed that he really doesn't have to understand much math in order to transform many equations, even those involving sines, cosines and logs, to BASIC statements.

****

BASIC MINI-LESSON:

In this chapter you learned that when the task is simply to have the computer print the answer to an equation, you type a line number, then the word PRINT followed by the equation. Operators which may be used in expressions are + (addition), - (subtraction), * (multiplication), / (division), and ↑ (raising to a power).

RUN is a *system command*. It tells the computer that you wish to execute a program you've typed in.

END is a statement which may be required on some time-sharing systems. If your system requires it, type

        99999 END

as the last statement of every program.

BASIC understands several functions including SIN, COS, LOG, SQR., etc. All functions require arguments enclosed in parentheses.

EXERCISES:

1. Write a BASIC program to give an answer to

$$44.8 + 8.63 - .007 = ?$$

2. Write a BASIC program to find answers to

$$\frac{67.43}{81.9} + 3.6 = \;?$$

and

$$8.34^3 + \log_e 1.3 = ?$$

3. Write a BASIC program to solve this equation

$$\sqrt{\dfrac{\dfrac{398.1}{4.6}}{\dfrac{14.9}{3}}} = ?$$

Chapter 3

LOOPS

You wouldn't use a computer to help you solve problems if some form of *looping* weren't involved. What is a loop? To illustrate, let's look at a frivolous example:

```
10  GO TO 20
20  GO TO 10
RUN
```

These two BASIC statements form a computer program, but as you can see, it's a do-nothing program. The computer is directed to jump from line 10 to line 20, back to line 10, etc. There is no limit to how long this program will run, so don't try it for practice.

Let's compose a more meaningful program which involves a loop. Say we have an equation:

$$(3.5 * Z)/2.5 = ?$$

and we want answers when Z is .1, .2, .3, etc. to 1.5, inclusive.

You can write a BASIC program like this:

```
10  LET Z = .1
20  PRINT (3.5*Z)/2.5
```

(Continued on next page)

```
30   LET Z = Z + .1
40   GO TO 20
RUN
```

The program consists of four statements. The statements are identified by line numbers 10, 20, 30, and 40.

At line 10, the value .1 *is assigned* to Z. Now, when the computer makes the calculation at line 20, the value of Z is understood to be .1 and the equation is solved accordingly. The result is printed out.

At line 30, the value .1 is added to the current value of Z and this sum *replaces* the value previously assigned to Z.

You can see that in BASIC, the equal sign (=) does not mean *equals*. It actually means *is replaced by*.

At line 40, the computer is directed to jump back to line 20 where another result is calculated and printed out. This time, the answer depends upon Z's value being .2.

We have a loop. The value of Z will be .1, .2, .3, etc. Each time a new value for Z is assigned, a new answer will be calculated and printed.

How long will the program continue? Unfortunately this program has no termination test (as there will be in future programs). Therefore, the only way to stop the computer is to do it manually. This can be done even if the computer is typing answers.

When the program has given you the answers required, hold down the *control* and *shift* keys on the teletype's keyboard with your left hand, then strike the letter P with your right hand. This will stop the program. Hit the letter P gently; otherwise, you may be disconnected from the computer. (On systems other than GE, you may need to learn a different method of manually stopping a program.)

Here is what the output from the above program looks like:

EX3-1   12:31   03 WED 01/13/71

.14
.28
.42
.56
.7
.84
.98
1.12
1.26
1.4
1.54
1.68

Admittedly, this is not a very sophisticated program. You may receive more answers than you want; you will have to stop the program manually; and the answers are not labelled.

Nevertheless, you can begin to appreciate the power of a loop. An amazing number of calculations can be made in a very short time. Consider this program:

```
10   LET R = 0
20   PRINT SIN(R), COS(R)
30   LET R = R + .0314159
40   GO TO 20
RUN
```

Can you see what the program does? It creates a table of sines and cosines from radian values beginning with zero and increasing in steps of .0314159.

Here is the program's output:

EX3-2	12:33	03 TUES 01/12/71
0		1
3.14107E-02		.999507
6.27905E-02		.998027
9.41082E-02		.995562
.125333		.992115
.156434		.987688
.187381		.982287
.218143		.975917
.24869		.968583
.278991		.960294
.309017		.951057
.338738		.940881
.368124		.929777
.397148		.917755
.425779		.904827

Again, when you've obtained enough entries for your table, you'll have to stop the program manually. In the printout, you'll see answers like 3.14107E-02 and 6.27905E-02. These are answers in *exponential* form. Numbers expressed in exponential form use powers of 10. Thus 3.14107E-02 means 3.14107×10^{-2} (or .0314107) and 6.27905E-02 means 6.27905×10^{-2} (or .0627905).

In the program above you may, if you like, change the radian step size to .00314159 radians instead of .0314159 radians. In fact, you can make the step size anything you please. Keep in mind that when the computer generates a

19

single point of your sine or cosine table, it works at a speed thousands of times faster than your own pencil-and-paper or slide-rule speed. Don't be afraid to give the computer plenty of work if you believe that work is required.

Did you notice that the PRINT statement in line 20 printed two answers rather than one? Indeed, you can have the computer print more than two answers. As many as five can be printed on one line of teletype paper, neatly spaced out.

Consider this example:

```
10 LET A = 200
20 PRINT A↑2, A↑3, A↑4, A↑5, A↑6
30 LET A = A + 1
40 GO TO 20
RUN
```

This program computes A^2, A^3, A^4, A^5, A^6 with A beginning at 200 and increasing by 1 to whatever value you wish to attain.

EX3-3   12:47   03 WED 01/13/71

40000	8000000	1.60000E+09	3.20000E+11	6.40000E+13
40401	8120601	1.63224E+09	3.28080E+11	6.59442E+13
40804	8242408	1.66497E+09	3.36323E+11	6.79373E+13
41209	8365427	1.69818E+09	3.44731E+11	6.99804E+13
41616	8489664	1.73189E+09	3.53306E+11	7.20744E+13
42025	8615125	1.76610E+09	3.62051E+11	7.42204E+13
42436	8741816	1.80081E+09	3.70968E+11	7.64193E+13

Observe how the answers are spaced across the page. You still have to terminate the program manually, but you'll soon learn how to have a program test for its own termination condition.

Note the answers in exponential form. 1.6000E+09 is
1.60000 x 10^9 (or 1600000000.). Since the computer is a
finite device, answers given in exponential form are often
only approximations. For example, the printout indicates
that 201^4 is 1.63224E+09 or 1632240000. Actually, the true
value is 1632240801. A computer can't always hold enough
digits to give you answers to a perfect accuracy. This is
no problem providing you are aware of its limitations and
are prepared to compensate for them.

****

BASIC MINI-LESSON:

The GO TO statement causes the computer to jump either
forward or backward in a program.

The LET statement is used to assign values to data
names. For example, LET P = 3 assigns the value 3 to P;
LET W = (D + Y)/5 causes the value (D + Y)/5 to be assigned
to W. Names to which you assign values are called *data names*.
A data name may consist of a single letter such as A, B, C,
etc., or a letter followed by a digit. These are correct:

X
Q
A3
P0

These data names are not correct:

AB (two letters)
A3B (too long)
3X (names can't begin with digit)

To stop a program while it is in a loop, hold down *control* and *shift* with your left hand and strike the letter P
with your right hand.

Answers will sometimes be given in exponential form.
This form involves powers of 10. Thus 9.41082E-02 means
9.41082 x 10^{-2} (.0941082).

21

EXERCISES :

1. Write a program which gives the square root of 1,2,3...
    Assume that the program is to be stopped manually.

2. Write a program which computes

    $$2500 \times I$$

    Where I is an interest rate which varies from .10 up-
    wards in steps of .01. Assume that the program is to
    be stopped manually.

Chapter 4

READING DATA

The examples of computer usage we've shown you thus far have, to a large extent, been contrived. We wanted to get you started with a minimum of instructions. Now we will begin to deal with more meaningful ways of using computers.

One of the most important concepts involved with computer usage concerns "input data." When you write a program, you solve a *general* problem. When you execute the program, you solve a specific problem by having the computer read *data*, the values actually to be used in the current situation.

An example will help explain. Suppose a department needs to know the circumferences of several circular pieces of glass needed in the manufacture of gauges. Here's a program which could be used.

```
10   READ R
20   LET C = 2 * 3.1416 * R
30   PRINT R,C
40   GO TO 10
50   DATA 9.8, 7.1, 18, 4.1, 20.4
RUN
```

The program *reads* a value for R (radius). That is, it refers to the DATA statement at line 50, picks up the first value there (9.8) and assigns it to R. The value 9.8 represents the radius of the first piece of glass.

23

Now the computer can make the computation shown at line 20. A value for C (circumference) is calculated using the value just assigned to R. (Circumferences are, of course, computed from the equation C = 2πR.). At line 10 the program reads another value for R, the radius for the second piece of glass. The program replaces the *current* value of R with the *next* value found in the DATA statement. The next value is, of course, 7.1. The program then calculates 2*3.1416*R, using 7.1 for R, and prints out the answer.

We have a couple of new concepts here. First, note that the program will continue to loop until the values in the DATA statement are exhausted. The program will then stop.

Second, notice the PRINT statement at line 30. You can print out values which have previously been assigned to data names. An alternate way of writing the same program is this:

```
10   READ R
20   PRINT R, 2 * 3.1416 * R
30   GO TO 10
40   DATA 9.8, 7.1, 18, 4.1, 20.4
RUN
```

This time, calculations are not assigned to C but are defined right in the PRINT statement. Either way of writing the program is acceptable. The answers are identical:

```
EX4-1              16:07       03 Mon 01/20/71

9.8                61.5754
7.1                44.6107
18                 113.098
4.1                25.7611
20.4               128.177
OUT OF DATA IN 10
```

24

The answers are not identified, but at least you can see which value of R gives which value of C. The program stops when it has run out of data and it informs you of that fact.

Suppose you wish to run the program again obtaining more circumferences for a different set of radius values. Would you have to rewrite the complete program? No, you would merely have to retype the DATA statement.

Here is an instructive sequence of events in another program: (The program computes not only circumferences of those pieces of glass, but also their areas.)

```
10 READ R
20 LET C = 2 * 3.1416 * R
30 LET A = 3.1416 * R * R
40 PRINT R,C,A
50 GO TO 10
60 DATA 2.9, 3.2, 8.1, 4.4
RUN
```

EX4-2	16:10	03 TUES 01/19/71
2.9	18.2213	26.4209
3.2	20.1062	32.17
8.1	50.8939	206.12
4.4	27.6461	60.8214

OUT OF DATA IN 10


```
60 DATA 16.1, 28.4, 200.1
RUN
```

25

```
EX4-2            16:11          03 TUES 01/19/71

   16.1          101.16           814.334
   28.4          178.443         2533.89
   200.1         1257.27          125790.

OUT OF DATA IN 10


60 DATA 414.38, 2.6, 17.1, 8.03
RUN

EX4-2            16.13          03 TUES 01/19/71

   414.38        2603.63          539447.
   2.6           16.3363          21.2372
   17.1          107.443          918.635
   8.03          50.4541          202.573

OUT OF DATA IN 10
```

Observe that it is possible to change a DATA statement simply by retyping it.

By now you must have several questions which we'll try to anticipate and answer.

First, can you read more than one value at a time using READ? Yes.

```
10 READ A,B,C
20 LET X = A * B + C
30 PRINT A,B,C,X
40 GO TO 10
50 DATA 1.5, 6, 7.2, 8, 8.3, 10
RUN
```

In this example, the program processes two cases. For the first, the values of A, B, and C are 1.5, 6 and 7.2,

26

respectively. For the second, the values of A, B and C are 8, 8.3 and 10, respectively.

When the program runs, the output is this:

EX4-3   16:15   03 MON 01/18/71

| 1.5 | 6 | 7.2 | 16.2 |
| 8 | 8.3 | 10 | 76.4 |

OUT OF DATA IN 10

What happens if there are not enough values in the DATA statement permitting the READ statement to obtain a *complete* set? The program stops. It will not try to work with only a portion of the required set of values.

Another question: Where is the DATA statement placed in a program? The answer is *anywhere*. Furthermore, you may place more than one DATA statement in a program. Example:

```
10 DATA 1, 2, 3
20 LET S = 0
30 READ X
40 LET S = S + X
50 PRINT S
60 DATA 4,5,6
70 GO TO 30
80 DATA 7,8
RUN
```

There are three DATA statements in the program. The program considers them as *one linked* DATA statement. They are linked in the same order that they appear in the program.

In this example, the three DATA statements could have been written as one continuous DATA statement. However, in some programs, there aren't enough character positions on one

27

line to permit only one DATA statement. It's all right to have five, ten, twenty or even more DATA statements in a program if they're required.

We suggest that DATA statements be placed either at the very beginning of your programs or at the very end (just before the RUN statement).

Here is the output from the example program above:

EX4-4   16:17   03 MON 01/18/71

    1

    3

    6

   10

   15

   21

   28

   36

OUT OF DATA IN 30

In the examples above, we invented data names R, C, A, X, S, etc., to which we could assign values. When you invent a data name, that name may consist only of a *single letter*, or a *single letter followed by a single digit*.

Here are some examples of legal data names in BASIC:

A, B, C, X, Y, Z, I, J, K, A3, B6, Q9, H0, R1, R2

A value assigned to a data name remains constant until changed by the program. See if you can determine the final values assigned to data names A1, A2, A3 and A4 in this little program.

```
10 LET A1 = 3
20 READ A2
30 LET A1 = A1 + 1
40 LET A3 = A1 + A2 + 1
50 READ A2, A3
60 PRINT A1, A2, A3, A4
70 DATA 8.4, 7.3, 2.6
RUN
```

Here's the computer's output:

EX4-5   16:18   03 MON 01/18/71

4   7.3   2.6   0

The value assigned to A1 was originally 3; later 1 is added to it, making it 4.

The value for A2 (8.4) was originally read from the DATA statement. Later the new value 7.3 was assigned to A2. The second value *replaced* the first one.

A3's value was originally computed as A1 + A2 + 1 but it was later replaced by 2.6, a value read from the DATA statement. The latter value *replaced* the earlier value.

A4 was never assigned a value. The program prints 0 (zero) for A4. Be wary of this. On some computers, a data name which has never been assigned a value may contain an unpredictable value.

The final problem in this lesson is to solve the equation

$$R = \frac{-b \mp \sqrt{b^2 - 4ac}}{2a}$$

For the mathematicians in our midst, we'd like to point out that the values of A, B and C have been chosen to insure

29

"real roots."

```
10 READ A, B, C
20 LET Q = SQR (B↑2 - 4 * A * C)
30 LET T = 2 * A
40 LET R1 = (-B + Q)/T
50 LET R2 = (-B-Q)/T
60 PRINT A, B, C, R1, R2
70 GO TO 10
80 DATA 1, 5, 2, 2, 6, -1, -2, -6, 3, -2, 8, -2
RUN
```

The output looks like this:

EX4-6   16:21   03 MON 01/18/71

1	5	2	-.438447	-4.56155
2	6	-1	.158312	-3.15831
-2	-6	3	-3.43649	.436492
-2	8	-2	.267949	3.73205

OUT OF DATA IN 10

Why does the program break up the equation at lines 20, 30, 40, and 50. Couldn't the program be written:

```
10 READ A, B, C
20 LET R1 = (-B + SQR(B↑2 - 4 * A * C))/(2 * A)
30 LET R2 = (-B - SQR (B↑2 - 4 * A * C))/(2 * A)
40 PRINT A, B, C, R1, R2
50 GO TO 10
60 DATA 1, 5, 2, 2, 6, -1, -2, -6, 3, -2, 8, -2
RUN
```

thereby saving two statements?

Yes, but the computer would then have to repeat the same sequence of operations more often than necessary. By computing and assigning a name to "b^2 - 4ac" and "2a," we save the computer some effort in computing. Saving the computer effort, saves money.

It's a small point, but it is the awareness of cost-saving techniques like this which differentiates between a mediocre programmer and a good one.

****

BASIC MINI-LESSON

The READ statement obtains values from the DATA statement. Examples:

    10 READ A
    20 READ X, Y, Z

The DATA statement provides values for a program. Example:

    80 DATA 14.6, 17.2, 81.8

The statement may appear anywhere in a program. There may be as many DATA statements as you require in a program.

Always provide complete *sets* of data. If a READ statement calls for 3 values, but there are only two remaining to be used, the computer will print OUT OF DATA.

EXERCISES:

1. The value, A, of an investment B, at the end of N years at I percent compounded Q times per year is given by the formula:
$$A = P(1 + \frac{I}{Q})^{NQ}$$

   Write a program which computes A using the values shown in the table on page 32.

P	N	I	Q	A
4163.85	3	.05	4	?
5000.00	10	.04	4	?
1000.00	14	.05	4	?
1000.00	7	.10	12	?
1000.00	1	1.00	10	?
1000.00	1	1.00	100	?
1000.00	1	1.00	1000	?

2. Write a program which will give the area of these rectangles.

LENGTH	WIDTH	AREA
14	65	?
18.1	47	?
32	76	?
13.6	18.3	?
19.2	11.3	?

Chapter 5

PRINTING HEADINGS & LABELS

In previous chapters, programs had no identification for answers. In this chapter you'll learn how to place headings on pages and how to label individual answers.

Let's compute volumes of spheres:

```
10 PRINT "PROGRAM COMPUTES SPHERE VOLUMES"
20 PRINT
30 PRINT "RADIUS","VOLUME"
40 PRINT
50 READ R
60 LET V = (4/3) * 3.1416 * (R↑3)
70 PRINT R,V
80 GO TO 50
90 DATA 2, 4, 6
RUN
```

Here's the computer's output:

```
EX5-1           13:09        03 WED 01/20/71

PROGRAM COMPUTES SPHERE VOLUMES

RADIUS              VOLUME

 2                  33.5104
 4                  268.083
 6                  904.781
OUT OF DATA IN 50
```

You can see that the message PROGRAM COMPUTES SPHERE VOLUMES was typed by the program beginning at the left-hand edge of the teletypewriter paper. The statement at line 10 caused the printing of this message.

There are 75 print positions available on output paper. The positions are divided into 5 zones (each 15 print positions wide). The zones begin in columns 1, 16, 31, 46, and 61. Unless otherwise directed, programs place answers beginning at these print positions.

That last sentence is not precisely correct. Answers are placed beginning at the positions shown if they are *negative*. Positive numbers begin one print position to the right. Look at the printout of radius and volume values. Radius values begin in print position 2 and volume values begin in print position 17. One print position is reserved for the minus sign, should it be needed.

Observe where the column headings RADIUS and VOLUME are printed. They begin in columns 1 and 16 respectively. The positioning of the column headings is not perfect, but you can see that it would be easy to improve. We'll do this soon.

What about the PRINT statements at lines 20 and 40? They cause blank lines to appear in the output. You get one blank line for every "blank" PRINT statement you write.

Now let's improve the column heading VOLUME. Type these statements:

```
30 PRINT "RADIUS", "  VOLUME"
RUN
```

Statement 30 in the above program has been changed and the program runs. Note that in statement 30 there are now two spaces between the quotation marks and the V in VOLUME.

34

These two spaces will appear in the new output. See below:

```
EX5-2            13:11        03 WED 01/20/71

PROGRAM COMPUTES SPHERE VOLUMES

RADIUS             VOLUME

  2               33.5104
  4               268.083
  6               904.781

OUT OF DATA IN 50
```

To *change* a statement, simply retype it. (You don't have to retype the whole program.) The computer will delete the old statement and replace it with the one you've just typed.

To *insert* a statement at some point in the program, choose a line number between two existing line numbers at that point and type your statement to be added. The computer will *insert* that statement in the place you've selected. (Now you can see why you should leave plenty of gap between line numbers.)

To *delete* a statement, type only the line number of that statement, then return the carriage.

If you want to crowd more than 5 answers on a line, use a semi-colon in a PRINT statement instead of a comma between data names.

Here is an illustration:

```
10 READ A, B, C
20 PRINT A↑2; B↑2; C↑2; A↑3: B↑3; C↑3; A↑4; B↑4; C↑4;
30 DATA 2, 450, 8192
RUN
```

35

The output looks like this:

EX5-3   13:14   03 WED 01/20/71

4   202500   67108864   8   91125000   5.49756E+11   16
4.10063E+10   4.50360E+15

The computer decides how many answers to pack per line, the smaller the number of digits per value, the more answers you get. Overflows are printed on the following line (or lines).

Finally, you can have the computer print on *one* line the results of calculations during sequential'times through a loop. Note this example:

```
10 LET A = 2
20 PRINT A↑2,
30 LET A = A + 1
40 GO TO 20
RUN
```

The comma following A↑2 causes the output shown below. You'll see that five answers are printed per line when a comma is used:

EX5-4	13:15	WED 01/20/71		
4	9	16	25	36
49	64	81	100	121
144	169	196	225	256
289	324	361	400	441
484	529	576	625	676

The program was stopped manually.

Now let's change the comma following A↑2 to a semi-colon. Type this:

```
20 PRINT A↑2;
RUN
```

The output looks like this:

```
EX5-5        13:17         03 WED 01/20/71
 4   9   16   25   36   49   64   81  100  121  144  169  196
225  256  289  324  361  400  441  484  529  576  625  676
729  784  841  900  961  1024 1089 1156 1225 1296 1369 1444
```

You'll see that answers are packed more tightly than they are when a comma is used. Again, the program was stopped manually.

We can have "labels" appended to answers. Note this program:

```
10 LET A = -2
20 LET B = 3
30 LET C = 4
40 PRINT "A= ";A; "B= ";B; "C= ";C
RUN
```

The output from the program is this:

```
EX5-6              13:19         03 WED  01/20/71

A= -2 B=   3 C=   4
```

Note that the literal messages

```
A=
B=
C=
```

are printed. Each literal message within quotes is followed by values A,B,C respectively, as called for in the PRINT statement.

Observe that a blank was carefully placed following each of the three "equal" signs. These blanks separate the messages from their corresponding numeric values.

Blanks could, of course, be placed ahead of quotation marks. For example, " B= " will further separate A= -2 from B= 3.

****

BASIC MINI-LESSON:

Literal messages you want the computer to print are enclosed within quotes. Example:

25 PRINT "THIS IS AN EXAMPLE"

"Labels" may be appended to answers by writing a PRINT statement where a portion of the instruction is within quotes and a portion is not. Example:

30 PRINT "A EQUALS ",A, "B EQUALS ",B

Commas between parts of PRINT statements cause 5 answers per line; semi-colons "pack" information more tightly.

Examples:

50 PRINT A,B,C
60 PRINT D;E;F;G;H;I;J

The single word PRINT following a line number causes a "blank" line to be printed.

To delete a statement, type only the line number of that statement, then return the carriage; to change a statement, retype it; to insert a statement, type the statement using a line number which is between the two line numbers of the statements on both sides of the new statement.

EXERCISES:

1. Write a BASIC statement which will print the words THIS,
    IS, THE, END beginning in columns 1, 16, 31, and 46 of
    the answer paper.

2. Write a BASIC statement which will print 10 asterisks
    beginning in column 5 of the answer paper.

3. Write a BASIC statement which will print the values of
    P, Q, R, S, T, and U on a single line.

4. Write a BASIC statement which will center the words COST
    REPORT YEAR-TO-DATE on a line. (Assume the line has 75
    print positions available.)

Chapter 6

You have seen that it is almost impossible to write a meaningful program without a loop. You have also seen that input data give your programs flexibility. In this chapter, we'll show that the ability of a program to take alternate courses of action depending upon changing data values, brings forth the fullest power of a computer.

Here is a program which illustrates the capability of a computer to make decisions:

```
10   LET X = 0
20   PRINT X,SIN(X)
30   LET X = X + .2
40   IF X > 2 THEN 60
50   GO TO 20
60   PRINT "END OF PROGRAM"
RUN
```

The statement at line 40 is a *decision* statement. The program tests whether X has reached a value greater than 2. (The symbol > means "greater than".) If X *is* greater than 2, the computer is directed to jump to the statement at line 60. If X is *not* greater than 2, the computer automatically goes to the next sequential statement of the program. In this example, the next sequential statement is at line 50.

Let's see what happens when this program is executed:

40

0	0
.2	.198669
.4	.389418
.6	.564642
.8	.717356
1.	.841471
1.2	.932039
1.4	.98545
1.6	.999574
1.8	.973848
2.	.909297

END OF PROGRAM

The program computes sines of angles from 0 radians to 2 radians in increments of .2 radians. When the program detects that a further increase in X (the radian measure) causes it to exceed 2, the program prints END OF PROGRAM and stops.

An alternate way to stop the program is to write the word STOP at line 60. The program will stop when all the required sines have been printed, but there will be no "end of program" message. Try this by typing:

    60 STOP
    RUN

The output now looks like this:

0	0
.2	.198669
.4	.389418
.6	.564642
.8	.717356
1.	.841471
1.2	.932039
1.4	.98545
1.6	.999574
1.8	.973848
2.	.909297

A decision statement begins with the word IF. Following are two values or expressions separated by any of six "relational symbols". The six relational symbols and their meanings are:

>	is greater than
<	is less than
=	is equal to
>=	is greater than or equal to
<=	is less than or equal to
<>	does not equal

Let's go back to a problem we discussed in an earlier lesson. We want to solve for R in the equation.

$$R = \frac{-b \mp \sqrt{b^2 - 4ac}}{2a}$$

A glance at the equation reveals that $b^2 - 4ac$ (the "discriminant") must be equal to or greater than zero before a square root can be obtained. The SQR function cannot take the square root of a negative number.

42

The program will have to test b^2-4ac before an attempt is made to solve for R. Here's the program:

```
10  READ A,B,C
20  IF A = 999 THEN 120
30  LET P = B↑2 - 4*A*C
40  IF P<0 THEN 100
50  LET Q = 2*A
60  LET R1 = (-B + SQR(P))/Q
70  LET R2 = (-B - SQR(P))/Q
80  PRINT R1,R2,A,B,C
90  GO TO 10
100 PRINT "NEGATIVE DISCRIMINANT",A,B,C
110 GO TO 10
120 PRINT "END OF PROGRAM"
200 DATA 3,5,1,1,2,3,2,1,3,1,6,3,999,0,0
RUN
```

Here is the output:

EX6-3   14:16   03 THU 01/21/71

-.232408	-1.43426	3	5	1
NEGATIVE DISCRIMINANT		1	2	3
NEGATIVE DISCRIMINANT		2	1	3
-.55051	-5.44949	1	6	3

END OF PROGRAM

Study the program carefully. At line 40, the discriminant is tested to see if it's negative. If it is, the computer jumps to line 100 where an explanatory message is printed. The values of A, B, and C are also printed for reference.

At line 20, the computer tests the value of A to see if the last set of A,B,C values has been read and processed. A "dummy" value for A, 999, is used as the "end-of-data indicator." Note that the last set of data (where A equals 999,

B equals 0, and C equals 0) is not processed. It is necessary to assign values to B and C in the dummy case. The computer would give an OUT OF DATA message if a value for A only
has been available.

New programmers sometimes inadvertently leave out important statements. Suppose at line 90, the programmer had not
thought to place GO TO 10. What would happen?

Let's try this by deleting the statement at line 90.
Type this:

        90
        RUN

Line 90 will be deleted, and you get this printout:

EX6-4   14:18   03 THU 01/21/71

-.232408	-1.43426	3	5	1
NEGATIVE DISCRIMINANT		3	5	1
NEGATIVE DISCRIMINANT		1	2	3
NEGATIVE DISCRIMINANT		2	1	3
-.55051	-5.44949	1	6	3
NEGATIVE DISCRIMINANT		1	6	3

END OF PROGRAM

It is obvious that the GO TO 10 at line 90 is vital to
the program. Every time you get a printout at line 80, the
program falls through to the print instruction at line 100.
The program gives the correct answers, then incorrectly reports that the discriminant was negative.

Remove the GO TO 10 at line 110 and the printout becomes
even worse:

        110
        RUN

-.232408	-1.43426	3	5	1
NEGATIVE DISCRIMINANT		3	5	1
END OF PROGRAM				

The END OF PROGRAM message is given before all the data has been processed. Let's replace the missing GO TO's and also provide a heading for the program:

```
90 GO TO 10
110 GO TO 10
2 PRINT "          PROGRAM COMPUTES ROOTS OF QUADRATIC EQUATION"
3 PRINT
4 PRINT
5 PRINT "   R1","   R2"," A"," B"," C"
6 PRINT
```

Note that replacement statements can be typed in any convenient order. The computer sorts them according to line number.

Let's ask the computer for an up-to-date listing of our program:

Type:
        LIST

Observe that the word LIST, like RUN, is a system command and does not have a line number. The computer lists the program as follows:

```
2 PRINT "          PROGRAM COMPUTES ROOTS OF QUADRATIC EQUATION"
3 PRINT
4 PRINT
5 PRINT "   R1"," R2"," A"," B"," C"
6 PRINT
10 READ A,B,C
20 IF A=999 THEN 120
30 LET P=B↑2-4*A*C
40 IF P<O THEN 100
50 LET Q=2*A
60 LET R1=(-B+SQR(P))/Q
70 LET R2=(-B-SQR(P))/Q
80 PRINT R1,R2,A,B,C
90 GO TO 10
100 PRINT "NEGATIVE DISCRIMINANT",A,B,C
110 GO TO 10
120 PRINT "END OF PROGRAM"
200 DATA 3,5,1,1,2,3,2,1,3,1,6,3,999,0,0
```

Now let's run the program by typing:

    RUN

This is the output:

PROGRAM COMPUTES ROOTS OF QUADRATIC EQUATION

R1	R2	A	B	C
-.232408	-1.43426	3	5	1
NEGATIVE DISCRIMINANT		1	2	3
NEGATIVE DISCRIMINANT		2	1	3
-.55051	-5.44949	1	6	3
END OF PROGRAM				

BASIC MINI-LESSON:

The decision statement begins with the word IF. Following is a relationship to be tested consisting of two *operands* separated by a relational symbol. Operands may be either data names, literal numeric values, or equations. Relational symbols may be >, <, =, >=, <=, <>.

Following the relationship to be tested is the word THEN followed by a line number. The computer jumps to the indicated line *if* the relationship is true. It goes to the next line in sequence if the relationship is not true. Example:

    20 IF A > B THEN 80
    70 IF 6 < (P * Q)/R THEN 95
    75 IF SQR(X) = SIN(W) THEN 150

LIST is a system command which causes your program to be listed as it currently exists.

EXERCISES:

1. Write a program which computes the square root and the square of N when N varies from 11 thru 20. Have the program print N, $\sqrt{N}$, and N^2 for all N's.

2. Write a program which determines which value is larger e^π or π^e. The value of π is 3.14159 and the value of e, 2.71828. (You may assume the values are not equal.)

3. Write a program which tells whether it is better to invest \$1000 at 6% for one year compounded quarterly or to invest \$1000 at 5 3/4% for one year compounded daily. Use equation:

$$A = P(1 + \frac{I}{Q})^{NQ}$$

Chapter 7

FLOWCHARTING

A flowchart is a pictorial plan showing how the computer
is to solve a problem. It shows the *procedure* the computer
is to follow.

In this book we're going to teach you flowcharting by
example rather than by lecture. Most of the problems and
programs we deal with from this point will include the corresponding flowcharts.

Before going into the whys of flowcharting, let's write
one which describes the quadratic equation program discussed
in the last chapter.

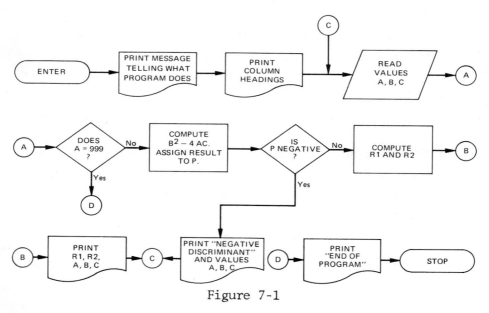

Figure 7-1

The flowchart clearly shows that two decision points are built into the program. It also shows what happens as the consequence of each decision.

Diamond shapes are used for decision points; parallelograms for reading data; paper shapes (curved bottom edges) for printing results; and rectangular shapes for initializing function and for making calculations.

Note carefully how loops are indicated. Arrows direct the sequence of computer operations. When the program must read another set of data, the arrows show a flow of control back to the symbol calling for the reading of more data.

The flowchart shows that headings are printed only once. It also shows that the message END OF PROGRAM is printed only once. Other portions of the program are to be executed several times.

We flowchart problems in order to make them easier to program. Much of the thinking about how a program is to be solved is done by a programmer as he creates and modifies flowcharts.

Of course a program may be so simple that no flowchart is needed. On the other hand, many problems are complicated and require elaborate pictorial representations.

Form the habit of flowcharting everything except the simplest of problems. You'll find that doing so will be difficult at first, but the task will become easier with practice.*

---

*   A good text on flowcharting is FLOWCHARTING by M.V. Farina, Prentice-Hall, Inc.; Englewood Cliffs, New Jersey 07632.

Chapter 8

LOOP ORGANIZATION

We said earlier that it is almost impossible to write a program without a loop. Many programs are patterned after this flowchart:

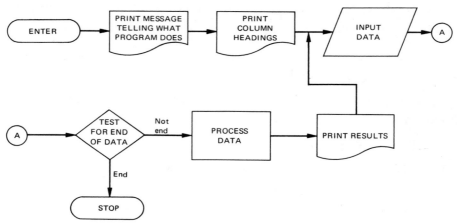

Figure 8-1

Check this example:

```
10   PRINT "PROGRAM COMPUTES AREAS"
20   PRINT
30   PRINT "R","A"
40   READ R
50   IF R = 0 THEN 90
60   LET A = 3.1416 * R * R
70   PRINT R,A
80   GO TO 40
90   STOP
100  DATA 6,5,3.3,8,2.2,0
```

In the program lines 10 thru 30 are *initialization* statements. Initialization statements are statements which prepare the program for the loop to come. They are not actually part of the loop.

The READ block of the flowchart is represented by the statement at line 40 of the program; the test for *end of data*, by the statement at line 50.

The *process* block of the flowchart is represented by the statement at line 60. In practice, the process block could be represented by hundreds of statements.

The PRINT ANSWERS block is represented by the statement at line 70 in the program.

The illustrative program will give 5 answers. When R is assigned the value zero, the program jumps to line 90 and the program stops.

There are three ways you can have a program conclude the execution of a loop.

1. Have the program run out of data values.

2. Have the program detect an end-of-data indicator, such as the zero in the example above.

3. Have the program count the number of times it executes the loop.

Except for the simplest of programs, it is *not* a good idea to have a program run out of values. When the program runs out of data values it will stop. If further processing is desired, the program could not do it. Example:

```
10 LET S = 0
20 READ A
```

(Continued on next page)

```
30 LET S = S + A
40 GO TO 20
50 PRINT S
60 DATA 6,5,4,8,2
```

If the system command RUN were given, the program would
not give the value of S. The program has computed the sum
of 6, 5, 4, 8, and 2 but it has not been able to reach statement 50 which causes the answer to be printed. A better way
to write the program is this:

```
10 LET S = 0
20 READ A
30 IF A = 999 THEN 60
40 LET S = S + A
50 GO TO 20
60 PRINT S
70 DATA 6,5,4,8,2,999
```

When you type RUN, the computer prints:

```
EX8-1            15:45      03 MON 01/25/71

   25
```

The value 999 is a *dummy*. When selecting a dummy value,
be sure to choose a value which will *surely never* appear as
one of the actual data values to be used by the program.

If you knew *ahead of time* how many times the main body
of a loop was to be executed you could have the program *count*
the number of times it has done so. Then, when the desired
number of times has been reached, the program could stop executing the loop and go on to the next part of the program.
Here is a portion of a flowchart, the portion which controls
the loop:

52

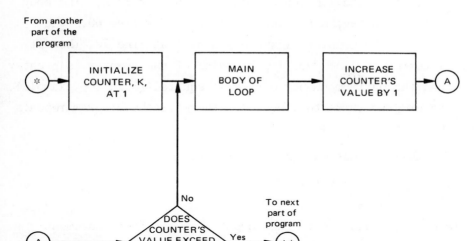

From another
part of the
program

| INITIALIZE COUNTER, K, AT 1 | MAIN BODY OF LOOP | INCREASE COUNTER'S VALUE BY 1 |

No

DOES COUNTER'S VALUE EXCEED MAXIMUM VALUE ?

To next part of program

Yes

Figure 8-2

As an example, suppose we know that there are 5 data values to process in a DATA statement.

```
10   PRINT "PROGRAM COMPUTES AVERAGE OF 5 VALUES"
20   PRINT
30   LET S = 0
40   LET K = 1
50   READ X
60   LET S = S + X
70   LET K = K + 1
80   IF K > 5 THEN 100
90   GO TO 50
100  LET A = S/5
110  PRINT "AVERAGE IS",A
120  STOP
130  DATA 346,321,516,412,457
```

In this program the name of the counter is K. The body of the loop begins at line 50 and includes line 60. The value of the counter is increased by 1 at line 70. Then it is tested at line 80. If the value of the counter is greater than the maximum number of times required (5 in the example), the program jumps to line 100, otherwise the program repeats the loop.

Observe that such statements as:

    LET K = K + 1
    LET S = S + X

are understandable to the computer. The first statement means: add 1 to the *old* value of K and store the result as the *new* value of K. The second statement means: add X to the *old* value of S and store the result as the *new* value of S.

The value of S is initialized with the value zero at line 30. It is good programming practice to initialize a data item if its value will be augmented during the execution of a program. If you don't initialize, you can *expect* that a variable's initial value is zero, but you may find that this will not be true for your computer.

A loop consists of four parts. They are:

1. Initialization of counter.

2. Body.

3. Augmentation of counter.

4. Test of counter.

Whenever possible, initialize a counter so that the *first* time the body of the loop is being executed, its value is 1; the *second* time 2; the *third* time 3; etc. The reason

54

for this will become more apparent when we discuss *automatic loops* in an upcoming chapter.

When you augment the counter of a loop, the step size is often 1; but it doesn't always *have* to be that value. Consider this example:

```
10 LET I = .02
20 LET P = 1000
30 LET A = P * I
40 PRINT A,P
50 LET I = I + .02
60 IF I > 1.00 THEN 80
70 GO TO 30
80 STOP
```

This program computes 2% x $1000, 4% x $1000, 6% x $6000, etc. thru 100% x $1000. There are 50 lines of printed output. The counter which controls the loop is I. It begins at .02 and increases in steps of .02 until its value exceeds 1.00. When I's value exceeds 1.00, the program stops executing the loop and jumps to line 80 where there is a STOP statement.

****

BASIC MINI-LESSON:

When a data name is shown on both sides of the equals sign, the *old* value assigned to the data name is used to compute the *new* value to assign to the same data name. Thus:

```
30 LET C = C + 50
```

augments the old value of C by 50 and assigns the sum to C.

EXERCISES:

1. Write a program which will determine which of three positive values greater than zero is largest; then print the result. For example, if the three values are 6, 8, and 3, the program will print THE LARGEST VALUE IS 8. The last set of values is a dummy: 0, 0, 0. Have the program test the first value of the dummy set. If it is zero, have the program stop.

2. Have a program determine whether the values A, B, and C given in a DATA statement will form a right triangle. Each triangle has this form:

A triangle is a right triangle when $A^2 + B^2$ equals C^2. In the DATA statement the order of the values is A, B, C, A, B, C, etc. The last set is a dummy (three zeroes). You may test A. If its value is zero have the program stop. For every triangle which *is* a right triangle, have the computer print RIGHT; for every triangle which *is not* a right triangle, have the computer print NOT RIGHT.

3. A DATA statement has 20 values. All values are either 0's or 1's. Write a program which will count the number of zeroes and the number of ones, then print the two results. The sum of the two results should, of course, be 20.

4. A DATA statement contains several values, all greater than zero. Some values are less than 1; some are greater than 1, but less than 2; some are greater than

2 but less than 3; and some are greater than 3. The last value, the dummy, is zero. Write a program which counts how many values there are in each of the four categories described above.

5. A DATA statement to be used in a program is this:

> 1000 DATA 10,8,4,7,2,9,4,6,8,9,6

The first number (10) tells that there are ten numbers following. These ten values are to be summed. Write a program which reads the first value of the DATA statement, then uses this value to tell the program how many values are to be summed. Have the program perform the sum calculation and print the answer.

Chapter 9

Many programs assign an initial value to a data name, then change that value as the program progresses. You've already seen this example:

```
10 LET S = 0
20 READ X
30 IF X = 0 THEN 60
40 LET S = S + X
50 GO TO 20
60 PRINT S
70 DATA 3, 8, 4, 9, 7, 6, 0
```

This program computes the sum of the six non-dummy values in the DATA statement. S is the name of a value which is initially zero, but which is increased while the program runs. The values assigned to S are 0, 3, 11, 15, 24, 31, and 37.

As the program runs, new values are *substituted* for old ones.

A more complicated program which uses the substitution idea is this one:

We wish to write a program which will compute $\sqrt{N}$. In BASIC this is easily accomplished by using the SQR function. Example:

```
10 LET P = SQR(8.6)
20 PRINT P
```

SQR is a built-in function which a programmer wrote. It computes square roots by using this formula:

$$G2 = \frac{G1 + \dfrac{N}{G1}}{2}$$

where N is the number for which we require the square root, and G1 is a *guess* that the program makes regarding $\sqrt{N}$.

The program then computes G2. If G2 is identical to G1, the computer has found $\sqrt{N}$. If not, the program assigns G2 to G1 and the equation is worked out again. When G2 and G1 are identical, the problem has been solved and G1 (or G2) gives $\sqrt{N}$.

Here's a flowchart which can be used:

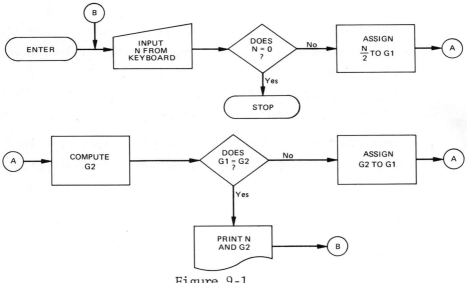

Figure 9-1

The flowchart shows that the initial value for G1 is N/2. This guess may not be a very good one but good or bad, the scheme will always compute $\sqrt{N}$, very rapidly.

Study the program on the next page:

```
10   INPUT N
20   IF N = 0 THEN 100
30   LET G1 = N/2
40   LET G2 = (G1 + N/G1)/2
50   IF G1 = G2 THEN 80
60   LET G1 = G2
70   GO TO 40
80   PRINT N, G2
90   GO TO 10
100  STOP
```

When you type RUN, the program will type a question mark on the teletype paper. You type a value for N and return the carriage. Example:

?34.7

The INPUT statement causes the question mark to appear. The computer will wait until you respond with a value. Then it will continue the program, computing and typing out the answer. Having done so, the computer will return to statement 10 and type another question mark.

This procedure will continue until you type zero. The program will then stop. Here is some output from the program:

```
? 34.7
  34.7              5.89067
? 64
  64                8
? 20004
  20004             141.436
? 984
  984               31.3688
? 144
  144               12
? 0
```

The critical statement in the program is found at line 60. If G1 does not equal G2, the value of G2 is assigned to G1. The value of G2 is substituted in place of G1.

Here is another example illustrating the substitution concept. Suppose you need to know which is the largest common divisor of two values A and B. You can have the program find this divisor by dividing the smaller number into the larger. Then the program determines whether there is a remainder. If not, the largest common divisor has been found; it is the last divisor used. If there *is* a remainder, the remainder becomes the new divisor. The new divisor is divided into the old divisor and again a remainder check is made. Here's an example: Suppose we need to know the largest common divisor of 36 and 64.

Divide the smaller number into the larger:

$$
\begin{array}{r}
1 \\
36\,\overline{\smash{)}\,64} \\
36 \\
\hline
28
\end{array}
$$

61

There *is* a remainder; therefore, divide 28 into 36.

$$28 \overline{\smash{\big)}\ 36} \\ \underline{28} \\ 8$$

There *is* a remainder; therefore, divide 8 into 28.

$$8 \overline{\smash{\big)}\ 28} \\ \underline{24} \\ 4$$

There *is* a remainder; therefore, divide 4 into 8.

$$4 \overline{\smash{\big)}\ 8} \\ \underline{8} \\ 0$$

There is *no* remainder; therefore, the answer is 4. The largest divisor common to both 36 and 64 is 4.

Here's the flowchart which can be used when writing the program:

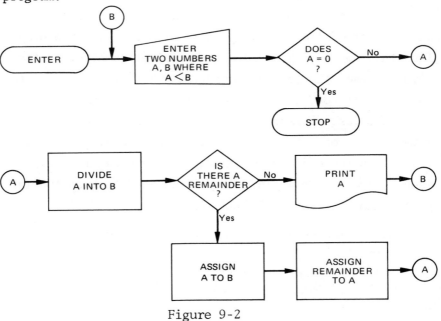

Figure 9-2

The tricky part of this program is how to determine whether there is a remainder. Study lines 30, 40, and 50.

```
10   INPUT A,B
20   IF A = 0 THEN 120
30   LET C = B/A
40   LET C1 = INT(C)
50   LET R = B - A * C1
60   IF R = 0 THEN 100
70   LET B = A
80   LET A = R
90   GO TO 30
100  PRINT A
110  GO TO 10
120  STOP
```

The INT built-in function extracts the largest integer from a value. For example, when C is 34.3, C1 is 34; when C is 34.8, C1 is still 34 (there is no rounding).

Suppose A is 36 and B is 64. The value computed for C at line 30 is 1.77777... The value computed for C1 at line 40 is 1. The value computed for R at line 50 is 64 - 36 x 1 = 28. This is the remainder. When R is tested at line 60, it is found to be non-zero, and the program makes the substitutions shown at lines 70 and 80. At line 70, the value of A (36) is assigned to B, and at line 80 the value of R (28) is assigned to A. The program is ready to make another division.

The program will always work regardless of what values A and B have. For example, when A is 7 and B is 11, the largest common division will be found to be 1.

BASIC MINI-LESSON:

The SQR function is used to compute square roots. These statements are correct:

```
10 LET R = SQR (38.7)
20 LET S = SQR (E)
30 LET T = SQR ((E + F)/(T-6))
```

The INT function is used to extract the largest integer from a given value. When P = 27.6,

```
40 LET W = INT(P)
```

assigns 27 to W. When P = 18.1 the value assigned to W is 18.

The INPUT statement causes a question mark to be typed on the answer paper. The programmer must respond by typing in one or more values as required. If more than one value is required, they must be separated by commas.

EXERCISES:

1. A DATA statement contains 25 positive numeric values greater than zero. The problem is to write a program which gives a 10-value "moving" average. That is, the first 10 values are to be averaged; then values 2 thru 11; then values 3 thru 12; etc. The last 10 values to be averaged are 16 thru 25. Have the program print all the averages computed (16).

2. Write a program which finds where the line represented by the equation

$$y = 5x + 6$$

crosses the x axis. (Have the program make a guess for x, then refine the guess until the solution is obtained.)

Keep in mind that the line crosses the x axis when y = 0.

3. Write a program which computes in how many years $1000
    will grow to $10000. The money is invested at 6% interest
    compounded 4 times a year. The equation to use is:

$$A = P(1 + \frac{i}{q})^{nq}$$

The values to be used are:

   A = 10000
   P = 1000
   i = .06
   q = 4

Have the program guess a value for n, then refine the
guess until the correct answer is obtained.

Chapter 10

FINDING AREAS UNDER CURVES

You will sometimes find it necessary to have the computer calculate the area under some portion of a curve. For instance, you may be required to find the shaded area under the curve shown here:

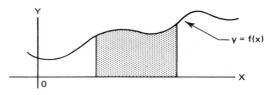

Figure 10-1

In mathematics, the topic of finding areas under curves is called *integration*. There are many ways to find areas under curves but most of those ways divide the area into strips, then sum the areas of the individual strips.

Let's investigate this technique by finding the area under the curve Y = sin (X) from X equals 0 to X = Π/2. Here's an illustration showing the problem:

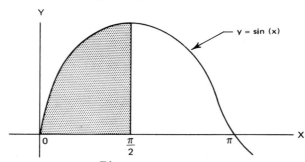

Figure 10-2

The next illustration shows a portion of the area involved and how we can divide it into rectangular strips:

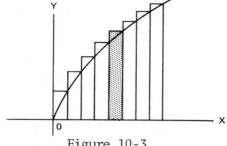

Figure 10-3

The shaded strip is one of the many to be included in
the problem solution. You can see that there is a small
area between the curve and the top of the strip which will
be included in the total area, making the area too large.
We must conclude that our answer will be only an approxi-
mation. In engineering, approximations are often acceptable. At any rate, we can usually get a better approxi-
mation to an integration problem by dividing the area into
thinner strips.

How many strips should we call for in this problem?
Let's choose 100 for our first try; then 200, 300, etc.

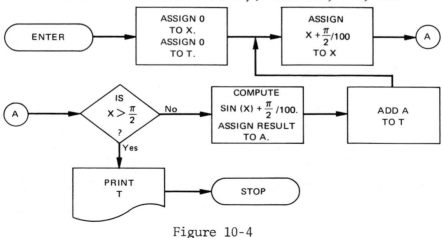

Figure 10-4

The value of Π/2 is a little larger than 1.5707963. We can safely round this to 1.5708 to test for *end-of-job*. It follows that the width of each strip must be 1/100 of 1.570 7963 or .015707963.

Whenever it is time to compute the area of a strip, we have the computer measure the height of the curve above the X axis (have it compute the sine of X), then multiply that height by the width of each strip. This gives us an area we can add to T. T *accumulates* the sum of the areas of all 100 strips.

Here is the BASIC program and its output:

```
10   LET X = 0
20   LET T = 0
30   LET X = X + .015707963
40   IF X > 1.5708 THEN 80
50   LET A = SIN(X) * .015707963
60   LET T = T + A
70   GO TO 30
80   PRINT T
90   STOP
RUN
```

EX10-1   15:16   03 TUE 01/26/71

     1.00783

This method of integrating is not particularly elegant; there are much more sophisticated methods in use. However, these results are reasonably accurate. Mathematicians will tell you that the actual area under the curve is exactly 1.

We can obtain a more accurate result by making the strip width half of .015707963. Let's try this by typing:

```
30 LET X = X + .015707963/2
50 LET A = SIN(X) * (.015707963/2)
RUN
```

The output is:

EX10-2   15:18   03 TUE 01/26/71
    1.00392

The answer is more accurate. In actual computer runs, the following table was compiled showing how the accuracy of the program varies with the number of strips:

STRIPS	AREAS
1	1.5708
2	1.34076
4	1.18347
5	1.14884
10	1.07648
25	1.03109
50	1.01563
100	1.00783
200	1.00392
400	1.00196
800	1.00098
1600	1.00049
3200	1.00024
10000	1.00007
20000	1.00003
30000	1.00001
40000	1.

The disadvantages of dividing the area into more strips

often outweigh the better results gained. More computer time is used, for example. (Doubling the number of strips doubles the amount of computer time used.)

After a certain point, increasing the number of strips offers no further accuracy. Indeed, accuracy begins to deteriorate. The computer is not able to hold infinitely small or infinitely large numbers. When we ask a computer to calculate using numbers near its maximum or minimum ranges, accuracy often suffers.

Rather than take a "brute force" approach where we just keep doubling the number of strips, let's look for a better integration method. Suppose we place the strips so that they are partially under the curve and partially outside of it. Study this next illustration:

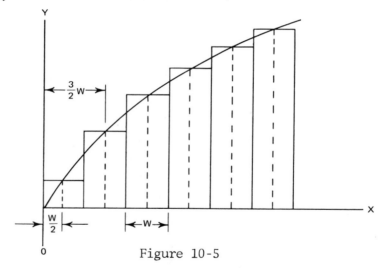

Figure 10-5

You'll note that the strips are partially inside and partially outside the curve. Observe that the width of each strip is W and is computed from $\frac{\pi/2}{N}$ where N represents the number of strips to be used. Observe also, that the area of the *first* strip is computed from sin(W/2) x W, the area of the second strip from sin(3/2W) x W, etc. The sines are com-

70

puted at the *mid-point* of each strip.

Here's one way to write the program:

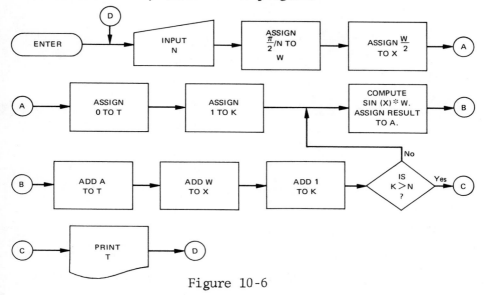

Figure 10-6

```
10   INPUT N
20   LET W = (3.1415927/2)/N
30   LET X = W/2
40   LET T = 0
50   LET K = 1
60   LET A = SIN(X) * W
70   LET T = T + A
80   LET X = X + W
90   LET K = K + 1
100  IF K > N THEN 120
110  GO TO 60
120  PRINT T
130  GO TO 10
```

The results given by this program are more accurate than those given by the previous one. Here is a table showing results using various values of N.

STRIPS	AREAS
1	1.11072
2	1.02617
4	1.00645
8	1.00161
16	1.0004
32	1.0001
64	1.00003
128	1.00001
256	1.

EXERCISES:

1. Compute the area under the curve $y = x^3$ from $x = 3$ to $x = 8$. Use the method shown above where the strips are partially inside and partially outside the curve.

2. Compute the area under the curve $y = \ln(x)$ from $x = 2$ to $x = 10$. (Remember that in BASIC, ln is written LOG.)

3. Compute the area under the curve $y = 3x + 2$ from $x = 1$ to $x = 5$.

Chapter 11

You may sometimes need a list of values to work with. You can establish a list by inventing a name for the list, reserving spaces for it, then reading values into it. Study the brief program segment which follows:

```
10 DIM A(10)
20 READ A(1),A(2),A(3),A(4),A(5)
30 READ A(6),A(7),A(8),A(9),A(10)
     .
     .
     .
100 DATA 48,14,19,12,14,25,20,18,22
```

There are a couple of new concepts in the example. First, observe the DIM statement at line 10. The word DIM stands for "dimension." Its purpose is to *reserve space* in the computer's memory for a list of values.

The statement shows the name of the list (in this example, A) and how long the list is (in this example, 10).

In your mind, picture list A as shown in figure 11-1.

Note that the DIM statement not only reserves space for a list of values, but also "initializes" every location in the list with the value zero. You will probably want to assign other values in those locations. That is what happens at lines 20 and 30 in the example. As you can see, those

73

lines contain READ statements. The execution of the READ
statements, causes ten values to be picked up from the DATA
statement (line 100) and stored in the ten memory locations
comprising A.

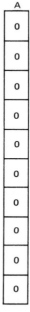

Figure 11-1

You'll notice that each READ statement gives the name of
the list along with numbers enclosed in parentheses. These
numbers are called subscripts. A subscript is a *pointer* to
a specific location in a list. That is, A(1) refers to the
first location in A; A(2), the second location; etc. Therefore, READ A(1), A(2), A(3), A(4), A(5) in line 20 causes
five values to be picked up from the DATA statement and assigned to the first five A locations. When the READ statement has been executed, the list holds the values shown in
Figure 11-2 shown on page 75.

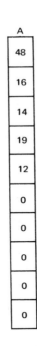

Figure 11-2

Similarly READ A(6), A(7), A(8), A(9), A(10) in line 30, causes five more values to be picked up from the DATA statement and assigned to the second five A locations.

When that statement is executed, all locations of the list A will have been assigned values and those values will be as shown in Figure 11-3.

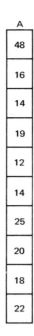

Figure 11-3

In the previous example, we showed that subscripts can be whole numbers such as 1, 2, 3, etc. Thus, when we mention A(3), we are referring to the third value of the list A; when we mention A(9), we are referring to the ninth value of A; etc.

Subscripts can also be variable names such as Q,P,T,etc. In other words, we can refer to A(Q), A(P), A(T) if Q, P and T have previously been assigned integer values such as 8, 3, 7. (Subscripts must always be whole numbers.)

The fact that we can use "symbolic" subscripts, such as Q, P and T, as well as numeric ones, such as 8, 3 and 7 permits us to use the powerful set of BASIC commands: FOR and NEXT. These two commands help automate the programming of loops. Consider this sample program:

```
10 DIM X(12)
20 FOR W = 1 TO 12
30 READ X(W)
40 NEXT W
50 LET S = 0
60 FOR W = 1 TO 12
70 LET S = S + X(W)
80 NEXT W
90 PRINT "TOTAL IS";S
100 DATA 8, 4, 6, 2, -3, 6, 9, 7
110 DATA -4, -7, 3, 5
```

In this program the name of the list is X. The DIM
statement in line 10 reserves twelve memory locations for X.

The statements at lines 20, 30, and 40 load the X locations with the twelve values found in the DATA statements
at line 100 and 110.

In line 20, the FOR statement gives the name of a subscript, W, and shows how it is to vary when the statement at
line 30 is executed. The value of W is to be *initialized*
with the value 1 and is to be increased in steps of 1 until
the value 12 is attained and used.

The statement at line 30 is therefore to be executed not
once but twelve times. The first time it is executed, W
holds the value 1; the second time, 2; the third time, 3; etc.
The *last* time the statement is executed, W holds the value 12.
During those times W will act as a subscript referencing the
first location in X, the second, the third, etc.

Each time line 30 is executed, a value is taken from the
DATA statement and read into a list location.

The *NEXT W* statement at line 40 is paired with the *FOR W* statement at line 20. Every time the computer sees that statement, it will increase the value of W by 1, then check that value to see if it *exceeds* the value shown in the FOR statement (in this example, 12). If it does exceed that value, the loop is completed and the program is to go to the next statement in sequence (in this example, to line 50); if W does not exceed the value shown in the FOR statement, the program is to repeat the loop once more.

FOR and NEXT statements provide greater flexibility in programming but programmers can have the program accomplish the same tasks without using them.

Consider the program on page 71 which computes the area under the sine curve from X equals 0 to X = $\pi/2$.

```
10 INPUT N
20 LET W = (3.1415927/2)/N
30 LET X = W/2
40 LET T = 0
50 LET K = 1
60 LET A = SIN(X) * W
70 LET T = T + A
80 LET X = X + W
90 LET K = K + 1
100 IF K > N THEN 120
110 GO TO 60
120 PRINT T
130 GO TO 10
```

The program could be written using FOR and NEXT as shown on page 79.

```
10  INPUT N
20  LET W = (3.1415927/2)/N
30  LET X = W/2
40  LET T = 0
50  FOR K = 1 TO N
60  LET A = SIN(X) * W
70  LET T = T + A
80  LET X = X + W
90  NEXT K
120 PRINT T
130 GO TO 10
```

At line 50, the computer is told that the value of the counter K is to be initialized at 1 and is to vary in steps of 1 through N. At line 90, the value of K is augmented by 1, *then tested* to determine whether its new value *is greater than* N. If K *is not* greater than N, the program executes the loop again extending from line 60 thru line 80; if K *is* greater than N, the program falls through to the next statement in sequence following NEXT K.

You can see that all the FOR and NEXT statements do is *automate* loops. The flowchart for a program is the same, whether it uses

```
        LET K = 1
   60      .
           .
           .
        LET K = K + 1
        IF K > N THEN 120
        GO TO 60
```

or

```
FOR K = 1 TO N
    .
    .
    .
NEXT K
```

On the left, below, is a program written using FOR and NEXT; on the right, the same job is shown without the use of FOR and NEXT.

```
10 DIM X(12)                         10 DIM X(12)
20 FOR W = 1 TO 12                   20 LET W = 1
30 READ X(W)                         30 READ X(W)
40 NEXT W                            40 LET W = W + 1
50 LET S = 0                         42 IF W > 12 THEN 50
60 FOR W = 1 TO 12                   45 GO TO 30
70 LET S = S + X(W)                  50 LET S = 0
80 NEXT W                            60 LET W = 1
90 PRINT "TOTAL IS";S                70 LET S = S + X(W)
100 DATA 8,4,6,2,-3,-6,9,7           80 LET W = W + 1
110 DATA -4,-7,3,5                   82 IF W > 12 THEN 90
                                     85 GO TO 70
                                     90 PRINT "TOTAL IS";S
                                     100  DATA 8,4,6,2,-3,-6,9,7
                                     110  DATA -4,-7,3,5
```

In both programs, the statements which begin at line 20 cause the computer to read twelve values from the DATA statements into list X. The statements which begin at line 50 cause the computer to add together all the values in the list. Note that in line 50, the variable S is set to zero. This is done to ensure that S begins with that value. When values are added to S at line 70, they accumulate there until the loop comprising statements 60, 70, and 80 (also 82 and 85 in one of the programs has been executed 12 times. The *last* value assigned to S is the one which holds the answer and must be printed out. This task is accomplished at line 90.

Since the statement in line 70 is executed twelve times, this means that the value assigned to S is *changed* 12 times. Satisfy yourself that the twelve values assigned to S at line 70 are 8, 12, 18, 20, 17, 11, 20, 27, 23, 16, 19, and 24.

When you run either of the above programs, you get this result:

EX11-1   8:15   03 WED 03/24/71

        TOTAL IS 24

A few important points should be brought out now. You may place as many statements as you please between the FOR and NEXT statements of your program. The loop defined by the FOR statement begins with the statement immediately following that statement and concludes with the corresponding NEXT statement. The loop is executed as many times as it is necessary to satisfy the conditions stipulated in the FOR statement.

FOR statements may be written in several ways. Here are some:

        80 FOR K = 8 TO 35
        85 FOR K3 = P TO R

In these statements, the subscripts are K and K3 respectively. Beginning and ending values are shown for them. In the latter example, K3 is to range from P to R inclusive. Both P and R must have been assigned values earlier in the program.

A *step size* can be shown for a subscript. Note this example:

```
105 FOR K2 = 9 TO 43 STEP 6
```

K2 is to be initialized at 9 and made to vary in steps
of 6 while K2 approaches 43. The values assigned to K2 will
be 9, 15, 21, 27, 33 and 39. The value 43 cannot be assigned
to K2 since 39 + 6 is 45, a value larger than 43. In the example, the largest value which may be assigned to K2 is,
therefore, 39.

Sometimes the step size is a negative value:

```
110 FOR K3 = 9 to -8 STEP -3
```

K3 is to be initialized at 9 and made to vary in steps
of -3 while K3 approaches -8. The values assigned to K3 will
be 9, 6, 3, 0, -3 and -6. The value -8 cannot be assigned to
K3 since -6 + (-3) is -9, a value less than -8. In the example, the largest value which may be assigned to K3 is therefore, -6.

The variable name shown in a FOR statement is *not always*
used as a subscript. Sometimes it acts as a simple *control
variable*. Note this example:

```
30 FOR A = .4 TO 1.6 STEP .2
40 PRINT SIN(A), A
50 NEXT A
```

This program will print sine values (for radian values
.4, .6, .8, ... 1.6) and corresponding radian values. The
step size, .2, shows how A, the control variable, is to be
augmented each time the loop is repeated.

In this example, A is not a subscript but as an *actual
value* which changes as the program progresses.

The control variable in a FOR statement can begin and
end with any required value. The following FOR statements

are OK:

FOR B = .8 TO 9.6 STEP .3   (The final value for B will be 9.5)

FOR X = -3 TO 8   STEP 2   (The final value for X will be 7)

FOR Q = 16 TO -6   STEP -1   (The final value for Q will be -6)

FOR S = P*3 TO Q   STEP R+S   (P,Q,R and S must have been assigned values when this statement is executed)

Don't write meaningless FOR statements. The following statements are not logical. Can you see why?

       FOR J = 13 TO -5 STEP 3

J begins at 13 and *increases* in value by 3's; it can never be -5.

       FOR K = -6 TO 20 STEP -2

K begins at -6 and *decreases* in value by 2's; it can never be 20.

BASIC will not execute meaningless loops such as these *even once*. The program will continue beginning with the first statement following NEXT J, NEXT K, or whatever NEXT statement is involved.

List names may consist of single letters only. You may have more than one list in a program. DIM statements must be shown in your program before the named lists are used for the first time.

Subscripts may be numbers such as 3, 5, 8, 20; names such as K, P, Q3, T4; or expressions such as 3*(P+Q), (J/W)*(W+3), J+6, (S3+W5)/M. The result of an expression's evaluation should, of course, be a positive integer equal to or greater than one. If the subscript isn't an integer, the

83

computer will drop the fractional part. The smallest subscript you may use is 1. This means that 0 and the negative
values are illegal when used as subscripts.

Incidentally, the summing program shown above could have
been written without the use of lists at all. Like this:

```
10 LET S = 0
20 FOR W = 1 TO 12
30 READ X
40 LET S = S + X
50 NEXT W
60 PRINT "TOTAL IS";S
100 DATA 8, 4, 6, 2, -3, -6, 9, 7
110 DATA -4, -7, 3, 5
RUN
```

The printout is this:

```
EX11-2              8:26            03 WED 03/24/71

TOTAL IS 24
```

This example doesn't mean that you'll *always* be able to
avoid using lists in programs. In the next chapter, we'll
show you several examples where they come in handy and offer
the only really convenient way to solve the problems presented.

****

BASIC MINI-LESSON

The DIM statement reserves memory locations for one or
more lists. The information you write following the word DIM
gives the name of the list and its size. Initial values assigned to all locations in lists are zeroes.

Example:

      130 DIM A(50), B(25), C(10)

Subscripts point to list locations. They may be either actual numbers, variable names, or expressions.

      1140 LET X(3) = 2.7
      1145 LET X(K) = 9.4
      1150 LET X(2*K+3) = 14.4

    The FOR and NEXT statements help automate loops. The FOR statement gives the name of a variable which is to vary its beginning value and its final value. Step size may also be given. If not given, the step size is assumed to be 1. The NEXT statement designates the point in a program where the variable mentioned in the corresponding FOR statement is augmented and tested. A jump is either made back to the beginning of the loop or to the next sequential statement of the program.

EXERCISES:

1. Write a program which reads 20 values from a DATA statement, then prints out all 20 values. Use a list and two FOR, NEXT loops.

2. Write a program which accomplishes the same job as Exercise 1 but which does not use a list.

3. Write a program which reads 10 values into list P, then stores those values in list, Q.

4. Write a program which reads 10 values into list P, then stores those values in list Q *in reverse order*.

5. Write a program which accomplishes the same job as Exercise 4, but which does not use list P.

6. Convert the following program so that FOR and NEXT are not used, yet it accomplishes the same task it did before:

```
10 DIM A(20),B(20)
20 FOR L = 1 TO 20
30 READ A(L)
40 NEXT L
50 FOR I = 1 TO 20
60 LET S = A(1)
70 LET W = 1
80 FOR J = 2 TO 20
90 IF S < A(J) THEN 120
100 LET S = A(J)
110 LET W = J
120 NEXT J
130 LET B(I) = S
140 LET A(W) = 9999
150 NEXT I
160 FOR K = I TO 20
170 PRINT B(K)
180 NEXT K
190 DATA 7, -9, 8, 9, 7, -3, 10, 5, 11, 6, 9, -6, 4
200 DATA 8, 15, 0, 13, 7, 12, 1
```

Chapter 12

USING LISTS

Before continuing with our discussion of lists, let's review the INPUT command, since some of the problems illustrated in this chapter require a knowledge of how that command works.

As you already know, when you use INPUT, you engage in a conversation with the computer. When requested to do so, you enter one or more numeric values. The computer does some processing and types out answers. Then it asks you to enter more values. Here's an elementary example:

```
1    PRINT "PROGRAM GIVES SQUARE ROOTS"
10   PRINT "TYPE NUMBER"
20   INPUT N
30   IF N = 0 THEN 100
40   IF N < 0 THEN 120
50   PRINT SQR(N)
60   GO TO 10
100  PRINT "JOB COMPLETE"
110  STOP
120  PRINT "CAN'T COMPUTE NEGATIVE NUMBER",N
130  GO TO 10
```

The program gives you the square roots of various N's which you type. Then it repeats the procedure until you type zero for N. You can see that the program checks N to see if it's negative. Since this program cannot compute the square root of a negative value, it prints an error message whenever you type a negative value.

Here is some sample output from the above program:

```
EX12-1                 9:42            03 TUE 03/30/71
PROGRAM GIVES SQUARE ROOTS
TYPE NUMBER
? 3
1.73205
TYPE NUMBER
? -4
CAN'T COMPUTE NEGATIVE NUMBER -4
TYPE NUMBER
? 0
JOB COMPLETE
```

INPUT statements can request more than one value. You can write a statement like this, for example:

```
10 INPUT A,B,C
```

When the computer types the question mark, you must enter *three* values. If you type less than, or more than three, the computer will politely tell you that you've made an error and will request you to retype the input.

Now let's return to our discussion of lists.

Suppose you want to have a program read 10 numbers into list A from the DATA statement, then *copy* into list B the numbers which are in list A. This is the program:

```
10 DIM A(10), B(10)
20 FOR K = 1 TO 10
30 READ A(K)
40 NEXT K
50 FOR K = 1 TO 10
60 LET B(K) = A(K)
70 NEXT K
80 STOP
90 DATA 3, 6, 7, 8, 12, 15, 21, 24, 25, 28
```

An alternate way to solve the problem is this:

```
10 DIM A(10), B(10)
20 FOR K = 1 TO 10
30 READ A(K)
40 LET B(K) = A(K)
50 NEXT K
60 STOP
90 DATA 3, 6, 7, 8, 12, 15, 21, 24, 25, 28
```

Let's make the problem more difficult. Write a program to read 10 values into list A from a DATA statement. Then have the program copy those numbers into list B in reverse order.

```
10 DIM A(10), B(10)
20 FOR N = 1 TO 10
30 READ A(N)
40 NEXT N
50 FOR T = 1 TO 10
60 LET B(T) = A(11-T)
70 NEXT T
80 STOP
90 DATA 3, 6, 7, 8, 12, 15, 21, 24, 25, 28
```

An alternate way to write the program is this:

```
10 DIM A(10), B(10)
20 FOR N = 1 TO 10
30 READ A(N)
40 LET B(N) = A(11-N)
50 NEXT N
60 STOP
90 DATA 3, 6, 7, 8, 12, 15, 21, 24, 25, 28
```

The next example involves searching a list for the smallest value:

```
10 DIM A(10)
20 FOR J = 1 TO 10
30 READ A(J)
40 NEXT J
50 LET S = A(1)
60 FOR T = 2 TO 10
70 IF S <= A(T) THEN 90
80 LET S = A(T)
90 NEXT T
100 PRINT S
110 STOP
120 DATA 8, 3, 14, 21, 7, 2, 11, 5, 14, 7
```

The variable S holds the smallest value. Note that the original value assigned to S is A(1). The program then checks all the other values in list A to determine whether any other members of that list are smaller than S. If so, the program replaces S with whatever smaller value it finds whenever it finds them. When the search is complete, S holds the smallest value in list A. In this example, that value is 2.

Suppose the program must also find the position in list

90

A which contains the smallest value. In the program below P contains that position.

```
10   DIM A(10)
20   FOR T = 1 TO 10
30   READ A(T)
40   NEXT T
50   LET S = A(1)
60   LET P = 1
70   FOR Q = 2 TO 10
80   IF S <= A(Q) THEN 110
90   LET S = A(Q)
100 LET P = Q
110 NEXT Q
120 PRINT S,P
130 STOP
140 DATA 8, 3, 14, 21, 7, 2, 11, 5, 14, 7
```

Note how P is initialized with the value 1, and how P changes when S changes.

If this were all there was to the problem, a list would not be required.

```
10   READ S
20   LET P = 1
30   FOR V = 2 TO 10
40   READ X
50   IF S <= X THEN 80
60   LET S = X
70   LET P = V
80   NEXT V
90   PRINT S, P
100 STOP
110 DATA 8, 3, 14, 21, 7, 2, 11, 5, 14, 7
```

Suppose you have list A containing 20 values. Write a program which will sum the values and print the average.

```
10  DIM A(20)
20  FOR W = 1 TO 20
30  READ A(W)
40  NEXT W
50  LET S = 0
60  FOR Y = 1 TO 20
70  LET S = S + A(Y)
80  NEXT Y
90  LET B = S/20
100 PRINT B
110 STOP
120 DATA 4, 7, 8, -4, 7, -2, 9, 4, 7, 6, 11, 23
130 DATA 14, 1, -5, 10, 17, 7, 4, 7
```

This program can also be written without using a list.

Here's a program which computes a *moving* average of 5 values. This means that our program must read 5 values from the DATA statement, compute the average, then print out the average. Then the program drops the first of the five values, reads another value from the DATA statement, and computes a new average. It then prints out the second average. This procedure continues until all values in the DATA statement have been processed.

This program is somewhat more complex than the one shown earlier in this text, so we'll first prepare a flowchart:

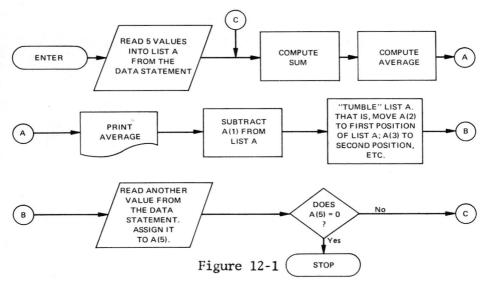

Figure 12-1

The program is:

```
10   DIM A(5)
20   FOR J = 1 TO 5
30   READ A(J)
40   NEXT J
50   LET S = 0
60   FOR J = 1 TO 5
70   LET S = S + A(J)
80   NEXT J
90   LET B = S/5
100  PRINT B
110  LET S = S - A(1)
120  FOR K = 1 TO 4
130  LET A(K) = A(K + 1)
140  NEXT K
150  READ A(5)
160  IF A(5) = 0 THEN 180
170  GO TO 50
180  STOP
190  DATA 3, 4, 5,-2, 7, 8, 4, 5, 3, 2, 7, 6, 1,-2,0
```

Here's the output from the program:

         3.4
         4.4
         4.4
         4.4
         5.4
         4.4
         4.2
         4.6
         3.8
         2.8

Suppose you want to write a program which will tell you the pressure exerted by a gas at some temperature. You can store values in two lists, one list for temperatures and the other for pressures. You must make sure that the two lists are synchronized. That is, pressure 1 and temperature 1 go together; pressure 2 and temperature 2 go together; etc.

Now, using INPUT, you can have the program accept a temperature value. The program will find that temperature in one list and type out the corresponding pressure from the other list. Let's see how this is done:

```
10   DIM T(100), P(100)
20   FOR S = 1 TO 100
30   READ T(S), P(S)
40   IF T(S) = 0 THEN 60
50   NEXT S
60   LET S = S - 1
70   PRINT "ENTER TEMPERATURE VALUE"
```

(Continued on next page)

94

```
80   INPUT X
90   FOR W = 1 TO S
100  IF T(W) = X THEN 140
110  NEXT W
120  PRINT "TEMPERATURE NOT IN LIST"
130  GO TO 70
140  PRINT T(W), P(W)
150  GO TO 70
160  DATA 8, 6, 10, 8, 15, 11, 20, 14, 30, 18, 45
170  DATA 22, 80, 26, 95, 30, 110, 40, 150, 52, 190
180  DATA 59, 212, 65, 0, 0
RUN
```

Here are the results from the execution of the program:

```
EX12-3                9:46          03 TUE 03/30/71

ENTER TEMPERATURE VALUE
? 10
 10               8
ENTER TEMPERATURE VALUE
? 7
TEMPERATURE NOT IN LIST
ENTER TEMPERATURE VALUE
? S
```

You'll notice several important points in this program. The first loop is set up to read in a maximum of 100 temperature and pressure values. However, as soon as the program finds that a temperature value is zero, it quits reading values. The temperature value, zero is a *dummy* value. The control variable S in the FOR statement at line 20 counts the number of temperature-pressure sets read in. When the program stops reading values, it has counted *one more* than the

95

actual number of values read in. That's why 1 is subtracted from S at line 60. Now S acts as a maximum value in the loop which begins at line 90. When you enter a temperature value for the computer to find, the computer will look through only S entries of the T list. If the program doesn't find the requested temperature in the T list, it will print a message to this effect, then request another temperature value.

When the computer finds the *exact* value of the temperature sought in the T list, it will print that value and also the *corresponding* value in the P (pressure) list. The subscript, W, ties the two lists together. Suppose, for example, that the requested temperature is found to be the third entry of the T list. W is 3, therefore, the computer prints the third value in the P list.

When you look up a value (such as temperature) in a list, you will often want to find it within a *range* of values. That is, you'll accept certain values plus or minus the one you're looking for.

As an example, suppose you are looking for temperature 38.2, plus or minus .5. If the computer finds any value in the temperature list from 37.7 to 38.7 inclusive, it will have made a "hit." You can have the computer search for a value within a range of values by writing an IF statement like this:

100 IF ABS(T(W)-X) <= .5 THEN 140

where T is the name of a temperature list and X is the temperature value being sought. W is the control variable used in a preceding FOR statement. In the example W acts as a subscript for the list T.

96

ABS shown in the example represents a built-in BASIC function which always gives a positive result. Thus if you have this statement:

    10 LET X = ABS(C)

and C's value is -8, the value of X will be 8. If the value of C is already a positive value, the value assigned to X will be that *same* positive value. The function's argument can, of course, be an expression or an actual numeric value as well as a variable name.

Note the above statement having line number 100. The ABS function insures that the difference between T(W) and X is always positive whether T(W) is less than, or greater than X.

Consider another example based upon an inventory situation. The program shown below has four lists. They are P (part number), Q (quantity on hand), C(cost) and S(selling price). The program accepts a part number, searches the P list until it finds the part number, then types the quantity on hand, cost and selling price:

```
10   DIM P(100), Q(100), C(100), S(100)
20   FOR T = 1 TO 100
30   READ P(T), Q(T), C(T), S(T)
40   IF P(T) = 0 THEN 100
50   NEXT T
100 LET T = T - 1
110 PRINT "TYPE PART NUMBER"
120 INPUT X
130 FOR W = 1 TO T
140 IF P(W) = X THEN 200
150 NEXT W
160 PRINT "PART NOT IN LIST"
```

(Continued on next page)

97

```
170 GO TO 110
200 PRINT P(W), Q(W), C(W), S(W)
210 GO TO 110
500 DATA 125, 60, 1.25, 2.10, 180, 45, .60, 1.05
510 DATA 195, 25, 3.00, 4.00, 0, 0, 0, 0
```

This program is very similar to the one which had only two lists. This one has four. Again, it is the subscript W which synchronizes the information you receive from each list.

The program has data for only three parts but it has been written so that it can handle 100 parts. The last part number in the DATA statement, zero, is not an actual part to be used, but a dummy which signals the end of the list. Note that not only must the part number be zero, but also quantity-on-hand, cost, and selling price. The READ statement in line 30 expects to pick up *four* values at a time from the DATA statement. If a *complete* set of four is not available, the computer will stop and give a message saying it has run out of data.

Here is some output from the above program:

```
EX12-4              9:52        03 TUE 03/30/71

TYPE PART NUMBER
? 180
180             45          6           1.05
TYPE PART NUMBER
? 125
125             60          1.25        2.1
TYPE PART NUMBER
? 100
PART NOT IN LIST
TYPE PART NUMBER
?STOP
```

You can stop a program at any time when it asks for an INPUT value (or series of values). Type STOP or S instead of the values requested. The program will terminate at once.

EXERCISES:

1. Write the flowchart for the program illustrated on page 87.

2. Write the flowchart for the program illustrated on page 89. (Bottom of page)

3. Write the flowchart for the program illustrated on page 91. (Bottom of page)

4. Modify the program shown on pages 94-95 so that it will search for the temperature value in list T which is closest to the one accepted from the keyboard (X). Then have the program print the closest value. You may assume that values of X will never be less than 8, nor greater than 190.

5. Modify the program shown on pages 94-95 so that it will search for the two values which bracket the X temperature value entered from the keyboard; that is, the value which is larger than X and the value which is smaller than X. Then have the program compute the theoretical pressure value based upon simple ratios between the three values. You may assume that values of X will never be less than 8 nor more than 190.

6. Write a program to compute the mean and standard deviation of 20 values in list A. Standard deviation is computed using the equation:

$$D = \sqrt{\frac{\displaystyle\sum_{i=1}^{20} (\overline{X} - X_i)^2}{19}}$$

where $\overline{X}$ is the mean of the 20 values and X_i is an individual value.

7. Write a program to convert 20 values in list A from temperatures in degrees Fahrenheit to degrees Celsius. The equation to use is

$$C = (F-32) \times 5/9$$

where C is the temperature on the Celsius scale and F is the temperature on the Fahrenheit scale.

8. Write a program to examine 20 values in list A. The odd numbers are to be placed in list B and the even numbers in list C.

9. Write a program which examines 20 values in list A and prints how many values are less than 10, how many values are greater than 10 but less than 20, and how many values are greater than 20.

10. Write a program to merge lists B and C into list A. Lists B and C are in sorted sequence in ascending order. List A is also to be in sorted sequence in ascending order. Lists B and C have 10 values. It is known that no values are larger than 1000. List A has 20 locations.

Chapter 13

EFFICIENT LIST SEARCHING

Though your methods may be inefficient, you now know several ways to search through a list of values. Review this program:

```
10   DIM T(20)
20   FOR S = 1 TO 20
30   READ T(S)
40   NEXT S
50   INPUT X
60   FOR S = 1 TO 20
70   IF T(S) = X THEN 110
80   NEXT S
90   PRINT "DIDN'T FIND";X
100  GO TO 50
110  PRINT "FOUND";X
120  GO TO 50
130  DATA 3,6,7,10,20,21,26,28,30,35
140  DATA 38,41,43,47,50,52,56,58,61,63
```

```
? 20
FOUND 20
? 52
FOUND 52
? 63
FOUND 63
? 15
DIDN'T FIND 15
? 35
FOUND 35
? STOP
```

In response to a question mark, the programmer types in a number. The program tells whether or not that number is in list T. Every time the user types in a number, the program begins searching at the *beginning* of the list.

You'll note that the data values are in ascending sequence. Suppose it was guaranteed that input values of X would always be in ascending sequence and that no values would ever be duplicated. Now we could modify our program so that every time the program searches the list, it begins at the point where it previously left off.

Here's an improved version of the above program:

```
10   DIM T(20)
20   FOR S = 1 TO 20
30   READ T(S)
40   NEXT S
50   LET B = 1
60   INPUT X
```

(Continued on next page)

```
70   FOR S = B to 20
80   IF T(S) = X THEN 120
90   NEXT S
100  PRINT "DIDN'T FIND";X;"PROGRAM ENDED"
110  STOP
120  PRINT "FOUND";X
130  LET B = S + 1
140  GO TO 60
150  DATA 3,6,7,10,20,21,26,28,30,35
160  DATA 38,41,43,47,50,52,56,58,61,63
```

When an input value has been found, the variable, B, is incremented by one so that the loop, defined at line 70, begins at a different location of list T, not always at the first location. If you try this program make sure that the sequential values of X which you input are in increasing sequence. This program has been written so that it *stops* if an input value of X is not found:

```
EX13-2              11:42          03 WED 03/31/71
? 3
FOUND 3
? 10
FOUND 10
? 30
FOUND 30
? 10
DIDN'T FIND 10   PROGRAM ENDED
```

If the values in a list are in increasing sequence, there is another way to conduct a search: a "binary" method. The advantage of using the binary method is that any randomly input value of X can be efficiently found. Here is a table

103

showing how many compares are necessary for various-size lists:

LIST SIZE	MAX NUMBER OF COMPARES
10	4
100	7
1000	10
10000	14

This table is difficult to believe at first glance but when you've studied the next program, you'll see why it works. If you're looking for a value in a list, you write the program so that it looks at the *mid-point* of the list. If the value desired is not there, you have the program split the difference from the mid-point of the list to either end and have the computer look again.

The program knows in which half of the list to continue searching because values in the list are in increasing order.

Suppose, for example, you have a list of 1000 values. You need to find value 320. Assume that location 500 of the list holds the value 676. You now know that the value desired, 320, must lie between locations 1 and 499, inclusive.

The process of dividing the list and making compares continues until the required value is found. If the maximum number of compares, according to the table given above, does not yield the number sought, the program must print a message accordingly.

Can you write a flowchart to show how a binary search is conducted? For simplicity, let's include only 20 values in the list. Write the program so that it has some meaning. Set up the data in the form of 20 *sets* of data:

$$C_1, Q_1; C_2, Q_2; \ldots\ldots\ldots\ldots; C_{20}, Q_{20}$$

104

where C is a catalog number and Q is a corresponding quanti-ty-on-hand.

Values of X, which represent random catalog numbers, are to be input one at a time. They are to be found in the C list, and the corresponding quantities-on-hand are to be printed from the Q list.

A flowchart which can be used in shown below.

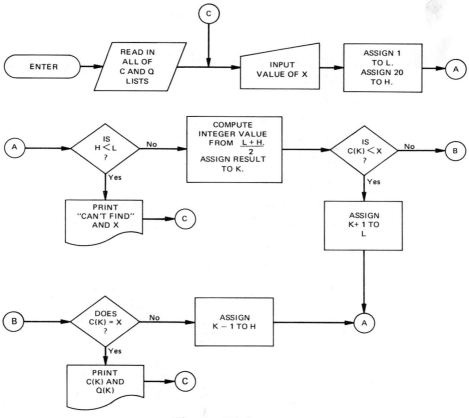

Figure 13-1

Now let's look at the corresponding program:

```
10   DIM  C(20), Q(20)
20   FOR S = 1 TO 20
30   READ C(S), Q(S)
40   NEXT S
50   INPUT X
60   LET L = 1
70   LET H = 20
80   GO TO 100
90   LET L = K + 1
100  IF H < L THEN 160
110  LET K = INT ((L + H)/2)
120  IF C(K) < X THEN 90
130  IF C(K) = X THEN 180
140  LET H = K - 1
150  GO TO 100
160  PRINT "CAN'T FIND";X
170  GO TO 50
180  PRINT C(K), Q(K)
190  GO TO 50
200  DATA 200,75,240,60,270,40,330,0
210  DATA 340,10,370,60,410,45,420,80
220  DATA 440,20,450,25,470,15,480,20
230  DATA 530,15,560,25,570,60,580,65
240  DATA 590,75,600,80,650,20,660,40
```

```
? 270
 270                    40
? 570
 570                    60
? 610
CAN'T FIND 610
? 620
CAN'T FIND 620
? 650
650                     20
? S
```

In order to convince yourself that the program works, you should go through a complete search "by hand" to simulate the way the program does it. Let's look for catalog 410. This is the 7th entry in the C list. It should take the program no more than 6 compares to find it.

Initial values of L and H are 1 and 20 respectively.

First value of K is INT $\left\lfloor \frac{L+H}{2} \right\rfloor$ = 10.

C(10) is not catalog 410. It is 450. H becomes K-1 = 9. L remains 1.

Second value of K is INT $\left\lfloor \frac{L+H}{2} \right\rfloor$ = 5.

C(5) is not catalog 410. It is 340. L becomes K+1 = 6. H remains 9.

Third value of K is INT $\left\lfloor \frac{L+H}{2} \right\rfloor$ = 7.

C(7) is catalog 410.

One final point: You can determine the maximum number of compares necessary to find a value by noting the size, S, of

107

the list. If the list is.

SIZE OF LIST	MAXIMUM COMPARES NECESSARY
$2^0 < S < 2^1$	$0 + 1 = 1$
$2^1 < S < 2^2$	$1 + 1 = 2$
$2^2 < S < 2^3$	$2 + 1 = 3$
$2^3 < S < 2^4$	$3 + 1 = 4$
$2^4 < S < 2^5$	$4 + 1 = 5$
$\vdots$	$\vdots$
$2^{n-1} < S < 2^n$	$n-1 + 1 = n$

Chapter 14

USE OF RANDOM NUMBERS

In this chapter we'll discuss the first of several problems involving random numbers.

First let's define random numbers. A random number is
a number that comes up completely by chance. There is much
argument among mathematicians about what is really meant by
the term *random number*, but we won't get into that. Let's
say, simply, that when you ask the computer to give you a
random number, it gives you a number the identity of which
you had no way of predicting.

The form of the statement you need to obtain a random
number is:

    20   LET P = RND(-1)

RND is a built-in BASIC function which obtains a number
between 0 and 1 (not inclusive) and assigns it to the variable name at the left-hand side of the equal sign. That number could be .234678, .947632, .014639, or any of many thousands of other numbers.

The numbers are completely unpredictable and satisfy
various tests for randomness. For example, in 1000 numbers
there will be approximately as many numbers between 0 and .1
as there are between .1 and .2, .2 and .3, etc.

To get a feel for what these numbers are like, let's

write a brief program which gives us 20 of them:

```
10   FOR Q = 1 TO 20
20   LET R = RND (-1)
30   PRINT R;
40   NEXT Q
```

When you type RUN, you receive this output:

EX14-1   8:16   03 FRI 04/02/71

.11403 .38839 .135124 .209946 .593568 .391704 .835065
.279365 .20727 .22254 5.58869E-02 .563025 .724666
.646523 .559309 .818738 .905521 .425372 .109004 .812129

You can see that RND is called into use 20 times. Each time RND is called, it gives a different random number. The meaning of (-1) following RND will be explained later in this chapter. For now simply use it as shown.

Random numbers can be used to *simulate* real-life processes. For our first simulation, we'll use the classical *lucky drunk* problem.

Assume that a lucky drunk is standing at the mid-point of a narrow bridge. The bridge, which is 40 feet long, spans a deep ravine.

Figure 14-1

The drunk staggers first in one direction, then the other. It is unpredictable in which direction he will stagger next. However, he is lucky, and every time he takes a step it will be either toward the left bank of the ravine or toward the right bank. He will not fall off the bridge.

Let's write a program to simulate the staggering of the drunk. Assume that every time the drunk takes a step it is one foot long. Have the program count the number of steps required for the drunk to arrive safely to either one bank or the other.

Let's do some analysis. Random numbers range between 0 and 1. Therefore, if you wish to divide the range of numbers into two approximately equal portions, you can assign all numbers less than .5 to one portion and all numbers equal to or greater than .5 to the other portion.

Now, suppose we agree that when a random number is less than .5, the drunk moves one step toward the left bank; when the number is .5 or greater, he moves one step toward the right bank. We can simulate the random action of the drunk by having the computer give us many random numbers. After each one is given, we can test it and determine how the drunk is to move.

Sooner or later the drunk will reach either the left bank or the right. Since we've counted the steps he took, we can print the total.

Here is a flowchart for the problem's solution:

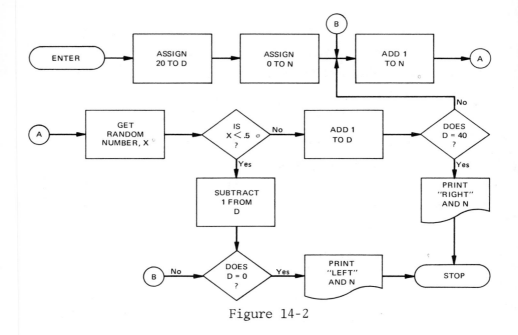

Figure 14-2

D is the drunk's position on the bridge. We've initialized this at 20 (the mid-point of the bridge).

N counts the number of steps. One is added to N every
time a new random number is obtained.

X is the random number.

Note that when D equals 0, the drunk has reached the left
bank; when D equals 40, he has reached the right bank. The
program knows which bank he's reached and prints out the
words LEFT or RIGHT, accordingly. At that time N is also
printed.

Here's the program and its output.

```
10    LET D = 20
20    LET N = 0
30    LET N = N + 1
```

(Continued on next page)

112

```
40   LET X = RND(-1)
50   IF X < .5 THEN 90
60   LET D = D + 1
70   IF D = 40 THEN 120
80   GO TO 30
90   LET D = D - 1
100 IF D = 0 THEN 140
110 GO TO 30
120 PRINT "RIGHT",N
130 STOP
140 PRINT "LEFT",N
RUN
```

EX14-2   8:20   03 FRI 04/02/71

LEFT   302

Note the STOP at line 130. It's absolutely necessary that the statement be placed there. Otherwise, if the drunk reaches the right bank, the two statements:

```
120 PRINT "RIGHT",N
140 PRINT "LEFT",N
```

will be executed. This, of course, will be wrong.

Naturally, executing this program *only once* is not very informative. The program should be run many times and the results averaged before a picture will begin to emerge as to the most likely number of steps required for the drunk to reach either one bank or the other.

Let's improve the program by changing it so that it will run over and over again until it is stopped manually.

Type this:

```
130 GO TO 10
150 GO TO 10
```

You'll get this:

EX14-3   8:30   03 FRI 04/02/71

RIGHT	808
RIGHT	164
RIGHT	72
LEFT	180
RIGHT	700
LEFT	274
RIGHT	124
LEFT	830
RIGHT	368
LEFT	1226
RIGHT	92

Now for a few details about the RND function. If the argument within parentheses is -1, you get a *different* set of random numbers every time you run the program. If it is 0 (zero), you'll get the same set over and over again. If the argument is a positive number, that argument is used to select the beginning point of a random number sequence.

Here's a program using zero as the argument for RND.

```
10   FOR K = 1 TO 10
20   LET B = RND(0)
30   PRINT B;
40   NEXT K
50   PRINT
60   PRINT "END OF PROGRAM"
```

114

When you type RUN, the output is this:

```
EX14-4              8:41        03 FRI 04/02/71

 .709245  .32882  .170769  9.08057E-02
 6.96426E-02  .212993  .75196  4.10837E-02  .56225
 .920782
END OF PROGRAM
```

Here's a program where an arbitrarily chosen positive number is used as the argument:

```
10  LET C = RND (5.6)
20  FOR I = 1 TO 10
30  LET C = RND (0)
40  PRINT C;
50  NEXT I
60  PRINT
70  PRINT "END OF PROGRAM"
```

When RUN is typed, the output is this:

```
EX14-5              8:43        03 FRI 04/02/71

 .273403  .741932  9.76314E-02  .571213  .518389
 .419873  .881379  .633618  .532304  .558149
END OF PROGRAM
```

Observe that a positive number is shown as the argument at line 10 and that zero is shown as the argument at line 30. The series of random numbers you receive are unpredictable the first time but you can rerun the program and get the same set of random numbers as long as 5.6 remains as the argument in line 10. When you want a *different* repeatable set of random numbers, you simply change the positive argument in line 10. That change need not be very great. Simply changing 5.6 to 5.60001 will give you a new set of random numbers.

115

The BASIC language makes it easy to obtain random numbers because RND is built into the system. When using the other languages such as FORTRAN, ALGOL, PL/I, you may have to obtain subroutines and incorporate them in your program.

****

BASIC MINI-LESSON:

The RND function gives random numbers between 0 and 1 (not inclusive). When the argument zero is used, the series given is always the same; when -1 is used, the numbers given are unpredictable and unrepeatable; when a positive number is given, the series is initially unpredictable, but it can be repeated as often as required.

EXERCISES:

1. Write a program which obtains 1000 random numbers. Have the program determine how many are less than .1, how many are equal to or greater than .1 but less than .2, how many are equal to or greater than .2 but less than .3, etc.

2. Write a program which obtains the average of 1000 random numbers.

3. Modify the lucky drunk program so that it'll run 20 times. Have the program average the number of steps required to reach either bank.

4. Write the program which answers the question: on the average what is the fewest number of random numbers which, when summed, exceed the value 1. To do this, have the program play 100 games. In each game, the variable S is initially given the value 0. Then random numbers are

116

added to S until S exceeds 1. In each game the program counts how many random numbers were needed to make S exceed 1. Have the program compute the average of the number of random numbers required to make S exceed 1.

5. Simulate 100 times a game between Pat and Mike. Pat has 20 pennies as does Mike. A coin is tossed. If it comes down heads, Pat wins a coin from Mike; if it comes down tails, Mike wins a coin from Pat. On the average, how many tosses will be needed before either Pat or Mike goes broke? Does the solution look familiar?

6. Write a flowchart which agrees with the program:

```
10  PRINT "I, THE COMPUTER, HAVE THOUGHT OF A"
20  PRINT "NUMBER FROM 1 TO 1000, WHAT IS IT?"
30  PRINT
40  LET R = INT(RND(-1) * 1000) + 1
50  INPUT X
60  IF X = R THEN 500
70  IF X > R THEN 400
80  PRINT "YOUR GUESS IS TOO LOW."
90  GO TO 50
400 PRINT "YOUR GUESS IS TOO HIGH."
410 GO TO 50
500 PRINT "CONGRATULATIONS."
510 PRINT
520 GO TO 10
```

Chapter 15

RANDOM MOTION IN TWO DIRECTIONS

    This chapter explores a problem in which we meet the lucky drunk again. This time we place him in the middle of a field and have him begin wandering aimlessly. We permit him to take 500 random steps, each one foot long, in North, South, East and West directions.

    We are interested in two things. After he has taken 500 steps, where is he and how often has he returned to his initial starting point? You are to write a program which simulates his trek. First visualize a field marked off like this:

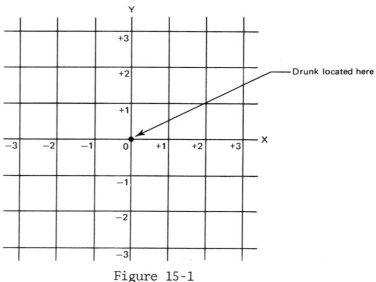

Figure 15-1

Imagine the drunk located at the point shown. We'll call this point 0,0 (X = 0, Y = 0). Define motion to the right as being in the +X direction; to the left in the -X direction; up, +Y; and down -Y.

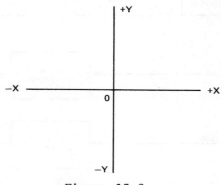

Figure 15-2

Any point that the drunk happens to be on can be expressed as a 2-dimensional address. That is, he begins at the point where X and Y are zero. If he moves to the right one step from point 0,0, his new location will be 1,0 (X = 1, Y = 0). If he moves down from point 0,0, his new location will be 0,-1 (X = 0, Y = -1).

We can simulate the drunk's motion by calling for a random number, then having the number determine if the first step should be up, down, right or left (North, South, East or West). We can note his new position, then repeat the process 499 times.

Each time the drunk takes a step, we check to see if he has returned to point 0,0. Every time he does so, we add 1 to a counter.

Here's a flowchart we can use:

119

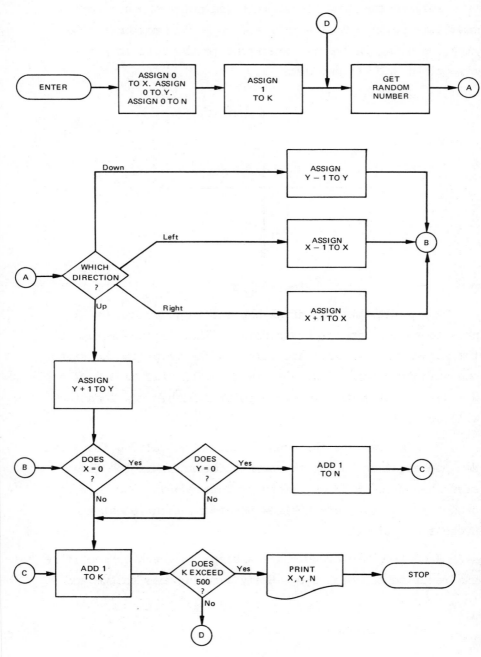

Figure 15-3

We've discussed the meanings of X and Y. K tells how many steps have been taken. The program ends when its value is 500. N tells how many times the drunk has returned to point 0,0.

How can the random number R tell us whether the drunk moves up, down, right or left? We can divide the possible range of values that R can take into four approximately equal parts, then arbitrarily assign directions like this:

$$0 < R < .25 \text{ UP}$$
$$.25 < R < .5 \text{ DOWN}$$
$$.5 \ < R < .75 \text{ RIGHT}$$
$$.75 < R < 1 \text{ LEFT}$$

Can you now write the program. Here's one way to do it:

```
10   LET X = Y = N = 0
20   FOR K = 1 TO 500
30   LET R = RND(-1)
40   IF R < .25 THEN 90
50   IF R < .5 THEN 110
60   IF R < .75 THEN 130
70   LET X = X - 1
80   GO TO 140
90   LET Y = Y + 1
100 GO TO 140
110 LET Y = Y - 1
120 GO TO 140
130 LET X = X + 1
140 IF X = 0 THEN 160
150 GO TO 190
160 IF Y = 0 THEN 180
170 GO TO 190
```

(Continued on next page)

121

```
180 LET N = N + 1
190 NEXT K
200 PRINT "X=";X, "Y=";Y, "N=";N
210 PRINT "END OF PROGRAM"
```

There are several important observations to be made in this program. First, note that at line 10, you can initialize several data items at the same time.

Then note the order in which the ranges of R are tested. If R is not less than .25, the program checks to see if it's less than .5. If it isn't less than .5, it checks to see if it's less than .75. If it isn't less than .75, then it *must* be less than 1.

Note how carefully GO TO's have been included at lines 80, 100, 120, etc. Erroneous results would be given if those GO TO's were missing.

When you type RUN, the output from the above program is this:

```
EX15-1        13:02        03 FRI 04/02/71

X=-12   Y=-18   N= 1
END OF PROGRAM
```

The drunk ended up in the field where X equals -12 and Y equals -18. He had gone back to his original starting point once.

A one-time run of this program is not very meaningful, so we can change it to repeat. Type:

```
210 GO TO 10
RUN
```

Now the output is this:

122

X = -23	Y = 1	N = 0
X = 6	Y = 8	N = 0
X = 22	Y = 28	N = 3
X = -4	Y = 22	N = 1
X = -8	Y = 20	N = 2
X = 30	Y = 4	N = 0
X = 22	Y = -2	N = 1
X = -2	Y = -14	N = 6
X = 26	Y = 4	N = 1
X = 14	Y = -2	N = 2
X = -26	Y = -12	N = 3
X = -6	Y = -28	N = 0
X = -2	Y = 0	N = 0
X = 10	Y = -14	N = 1

The program is stopped manually.

If we increase the number of steps we permit the wandering drunk to take, the output changes:

```
20 FOR K = 1 TO 5000
```

Now, the drunk takes 5000 steps instead of 500 and the results are these:

X = 11	Y = 3	N = 3
X = -54	Y = 2	N = 0
X = 14	Y = 18	N = 30
X = -22	Y = -60	N = 0
X = -30	Y = -100	N = 2

Another change:

```
20 FOR K = 1 TO 20000
```

He now takes 20000 steps instead of 5000:

X = 107	Y = 21	N = 0
X = 219	Y = -27	N = 1
X = -47	Y = 73	N = 0
X = 50	Y = 48	N = 1

We can improve the wandering drunk problem but first you'll have to learn how to convert a random number to an integer. Study this sequence of statements:

```
LET R = RND(-1)
LET R = R * 4
LET R = INT(R)
LET R = R + 1
```

These statements convert a random number to integers 1, 2, 3, or 4. The function INT extracts the largest integer from any given value.

As an example, let's test the method for when R is .42. Four times .42 is 1.68. The largest integer in 1.68 is 1. Adding 1 to 1 gives 2. Therefore, R is assigned the value 2.

Another example: suppose the random number is .9. Four times .9 is 3.6. The largest integer is 3 and 3 + 1 gives the final integer 4.

The four statements given above can be compressed into one BASIC statement.

```
LET R = INT(RND(-1) * 4) + 1
```

This statement will always give an integer varying from 1 to N where N is the multiplier shown. (In the example, N is 4.)

The ability to convert a random number to an integer

permits us to use the ON feature of BASIC. The ON statement looks like this:

ON R GO TO 50, 55, 60, 65

The computer tests R which it expects to be an integer. If R is 1, the computer jumps to line 50; if it is 2, the computer jumps to line 55; if 3, to line 60; and if 4, to line 65. If R is not 1, 2, 3, or 4, the computer will give an error message.

Other ways to use the ON feature are these:

ON A * B GO TO 10, 20, 30

ON P GO TO 6, 8, 6, 10, 20, 5

You can see that more than four line numbers can be shown in an ON statement. Some of those line numbers may be duplicates.

In the first example, it's assumed that A * B gives an integer 1, 2, or 3. If it doesn't, the computer obtains the largest integer in the expression's value and uses that value.

We can use the ON feature in our wandering drunk problem like this:

```
10    LET X = Y = N = 0
20    FOR K = 1 TO 500
30    ON INT (RND(-1) *4) + 1 GO TO 40, 60, 80, 100
40    LET X = X - 1
50    GO TO 110
60    LET Y = Y + 1
70    GO TO 110
80    LET Y = Y -1
90    GO TO 110
100   LET X = X + 1
```

(Continued on next page)

```
110 IF X <> 0 THEN 140
120 IF Y <> 0 THEN 140
130 LET N = N + 1
140 NEXT K
150 PRINT "X=";X, "Y=";Y, "N=";N
160 PRINT "END OF PROGRAM"
```

If you prefer, the statement on line 30 can be broken into two statements:

```
30  LET Q = INT (RND(-1) * 4) + 1
35  ON P GO TO 40, 60, 80, 100
```

****

BASIC MINI-LESSON:

When you need to convert a random number to an integer within some range of integers, use a statement having this pattern:

```
LET X = INT (RND(-1) * N) + B
```

where N is the number of integers in the range and B is the first of the integers in the range. This, if you needed integers ranging from 10 to 23, you'd use the statement:

```
LET X = INT (RND(-1) * 14) + 10
```

The ON statement permits multiple branching.

```
ON P GO TO 30, 40, 70
```

will cause the computer to jump to line 30 when P has the value 1; to line 40 when it has the value 2; to line 70 when it has the value 3.

EXERCISES:

1. Write the BASIC statement necessary to convert a random number to an integer within the range of 5 to 15, inclusive.

2. Write a program which causes the lucky drunk to wander about in a field. Have him take 500 steps but confine his tour so that X and Y will never be less than -20 nor more than +20. The program is to test whether the drunk tries to overstep these boundries. If so, the illegal move is rejected and not counted. The program must then obtain another random number in an attempt to make a move which is legal. (Walk begins where X=0, Y=0) Have the program print the final position.

3. Write a program which simulates the movements of a white knight and a black knight on a chessboard. For those who don't know how a knight moves, consider this chessboard:

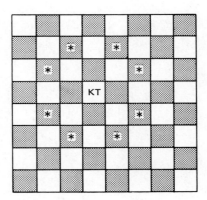

Figure 15-4

127

If the knight is located where shown, he can jump to
any of the eight squares containing asterisks. A knight
moves in an L shape, two squares in one direction and
one in the other perpendicular to it.

Assume the initial location of the white knight is in
the upper left-hand corner, and the initial location of
the black knight is in the lower right-hand corner.
Move the knights at random until they collide. That is,
until they both try to land in the same square. Have
your program tell where that square is and how many
jumps were taken by either the white or black knights.
A move is not to be counted unless *both* knights have
made legal moves.

Chapter 16

SIMULATIONS

In previous chapters we introduced a lucky drunk who staggers on a bridge or who goes wandering around on an open field. Let's bring him back along with forty-nine friends.

Fifty drunks have registered in fifty rooms of a hotel. After a particularly wild night on the town, they return one by one to the hotel, intending to go to bed.

Each drunk opens a door *at random*. If he finds the room empty, he goes in, drops into bed, and immediately goes to sleep. If the room is occupied, the drunk selects another room and repeats the procedure. (It is possible for a drunk to randomly select the same room over and over again.)

The problem: How many times will doors be opened before all fifty drunks have found a place to sleep?

The problem can be solved using formulas, but let's assume you don't know them. Let's, therefore, simulate the entire occurrence using random numbers. Print out the number of times doors are opened. Then, simulate again. See if the answers form any sort of pattern. We'll need a flowchart:

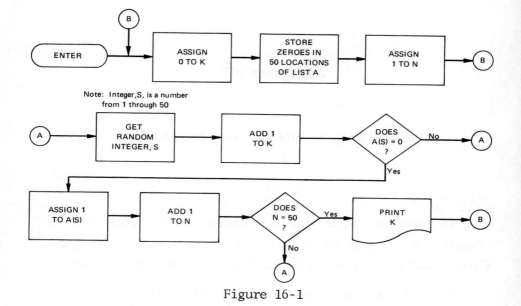

Figure 16-1

K counts the number of times a hotel door is opened. N counts the number of drunks who have found a place to sleep. One simulation is over when N equals 50.

The program determines whether a room is occupied or not by testing the corresponding location of a 50-element list. In the example, the list is A. When the contents of a location of the list is 0, the room is empty; when 1, it is full. Note that as soon as the program finds an empty room, it immediately sets the corresponding list location to 1 so that the room will be considered occupied.

Now the program:

```
10   DIM A(50)
20   LET K = 0
30   FOR I = 1 TO 50
40   LET A(I) = 0
50   NEXT I
60   FOR N = 1 TO 50
```

(Continued on next page)

130

```
70  LET S = INT(RND(-1) * 50) + 1
80  LET K = K + 1
90  IF A(S) = 0 THEN 110
100 GO TO 70
110 LET A(S) = 1
120 NEXT N
130 PRINT K;
140 GO TO 20
RUN
```

The program has to be stopped manually. The output
looks like this:

EX16-1   8:04   03 TUE 04/06/71

211	175	310	224	251	187	252	145	274
253	336	298	225	283	325	207	173	257
214	205	209	364	283	238	217	255

There are 26 simulations shown. You can see that the
range of the answers is from 145 to 364.

This would be a better program if it could deal with
more or less than fifty drunks. Let's make the program more
general by requiring the user to enter the number of drunks,
less than or equal to 1000. The program can be changed by
typing these statements:

```
0   PRINT "ENTER NUMBER OF DRUNKS"
1   PRINT
2   INPUT Z
10  DIM A(1000)
30  FOR I = 1 TO Z
60  FOR N = 1 TO Z
70  LET S = INT(RND(-1) * Z) + 1
LIST
```

```
0    PRINT "ENTER NUMBER OF DRUNKS"
1    PRINT
2    INPUT Z
10   DIM A(1000)
20   LET K = 0
30   FOR I = 1 TO Z
40   LET A(I) = 0
50   NEXT I
60   FOR N = 1 TO Z
70   LET S = INT(RND(-1) * Z) + 1
80   LET K = K + 1
90   IF A(S) = 0 THEN 110
100  GO TO 70
110  LET A(S) = 1
120  NEXT N
130  PRINT K;
140  GO TO 20
```

And some sample runs:

EX16-2   8:08   03 TUE 04/06/71

ENTER NUMBER OF DRUNKS

? 10

35	45	31	31	35	29	33	26	31	32
19	15	27	42	29	32	23	15	18	18
14	25	31	36	24	29	19	50	36	55
36	35	40	21	27	21	16	30	34	29
38	30	41	20	26	12	34	24		

132

ENTER NUMBER OF DRUNKS

? 100

381	423	558	845	458	465	724	764	635
517	698	606	548	497	607	589	406	546
447	427	503	441	360	533	544	921	742
438	723	478	409	454	640	469	456	430
636	465	372	394	482	419	626	556	480
516	480	516	655	412	357			

You might want the program to average its own results as it computes them. Let's introduce some new variables. T will contain the total number of door openings for all simulations; M will contain the number of simulations; L will contain the average number of door openings per simulation.

Let's add these statements:

```
5   LET T = M = 0
125 LET T = T + K
126 LET M = M + 1
127 LET L = T/M
130 PRINT K;L,
```

This is the new program:

```
0   PRINT "ENTER NUMBER OF DRUNKS"
1   PRINT
2   INPUT Z
5   LET T = M = 0
10  DIM A(1000)
20  LET K = 0
30  FOR I = 1 TO Z
40  LET A(I) = 0
```

(Continued on next page)

133

```
50   NEXT I
60   FOR N = 1 TO Z
70   LET S = INT(RND(-1) * Z) + 1
80   LET K = K + 1
90   IF A(S) = THEN 110
100  GO TO 70
110  LET A(S) = 1
120  NEXT N
125  LET T = T + K
126  LET M = M + 1
127  LET L = T/M
130  PRINT K;L,
140  GO TO 20
```

And some output:

EX16-4   8:13   03 TUE 04/06/71

ENTER NUMBER OF DRUNKS
? 25

82	82		85	83.5	97	88	114	94.5		57	87
117	92	64	88		83	87.375	149	94.2222	91	93.9	
90	93.5455	78	92.25		67	90.3077	96	90.7143	83	90.2	
137	93.125	66	91.5294		59	89.7222	89	89.6842	71	88.75	

EX16-5   8:15   03 TUE 04/06/71

ENTER NUMBER OF DRUNKS
? 50

144	144	211	177.5	189	181.333	189	183.25	200	186.6
326	209.833	205	209.143	218	210.25	265	216.333	167	211.4
363	225.182	304	231.75	189	228.462				

ENTER NUMBER OF DRUNKS

? 1000

5919 5919 9183 7551 8741 7947.67 5280 7280.75 7146 72538

In each instance every set of two values contains the current total and the average of all the totals, in that order.

Possibly you might want to plot these results.

AREAS UNDER CURVES

In emergencies random numbers can be used to compute area under a curve. Suppose it is required to find the area under the curve shown below where the equation of the curve is known:

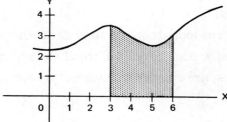

Figure 16-2

Let's put a box about the portion of the curve we're interested in.

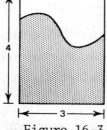

Figure 16-3

135

The area of the box can be computed since we know it is 3 units wide and 4 units high.

Now let's have the computer randomly throw several hundred points within the box. Some of the points will be below the curve, some above and some right on the curve.

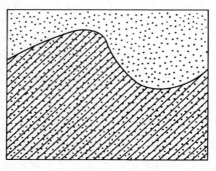

Figure 16-4

It would be reasonable to assume that the ratio of points falling below the curve to total points is approximately the same as area under thé curve to total area of the box.

We can write a program which will sprinkle points at random then count the number of them which fall below the curve. Then using the equation:

$$A = \frac{S}{N} \times 12$$

where S is the number of points below the curve and N is the total number of points, we can compute an *approximate* area under the curve. In the equation, 12, of course, is the total area within the box.

To illustrate how random numbers can be used for this

136

purpose let's consider a problem we've solved in an earlier
chapter. We want to know the area under the sine curve from
X = 0 to X = $\frac{\pi}{4}$.

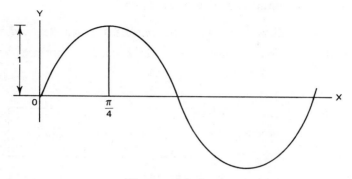

Figure 16-5

We can see that the area of the box is 3.145927/2. Now
let's sprinkle 100 points at random within the box. Each
point is defined by two random numbers; the distance along
the X axis by RND(-1) * (3.1415927/2) and the distance along
the Y axis by RND(-1). (We'll disregard the fact that a random number can never be zero or 1.) Having defined a single
point, we can test it to determine whether or not it's under
the curve by computing the sine of X at the X coordinate of
the point. If the sine of X is greater than Y, the point is
under the curve. See the figure below:

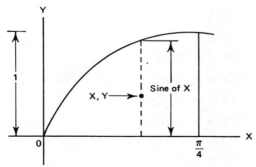

Figure 16-6

137

If the point is under the curve we add 1 to S, if not, we leave S unchanged. Following the same procedure with 99 more points, we'll accumulate a total value of S which can be used in the equation given earlier.

Here is a flowchart for the problem solution and the BASIC program. Also shown are solutions for various values of N.

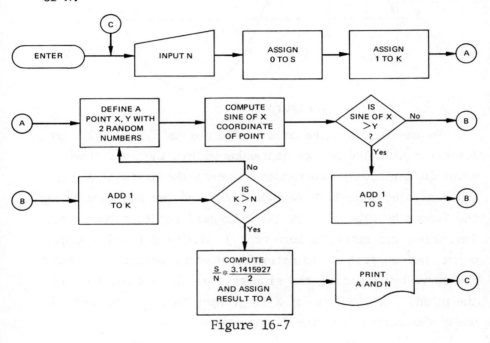

Figure 16-7

```
10   INPUT N
20   LET S = 0
30   FOR K = 1 TO N
40   LET X = RND(-1) * (3.1415927/2)
50   LET Y = RND(-1)
60   LET Q = SIN(X)
70   IF Q > Y THEN 90
80   GO TO 100
90   LET S = S + 1              (Continued on next page)
```

138

```
100  NEXT K
110  LET A = (S/N) * (3.1415927/2)
120  PRINT A
130  GO TO 10
RUN
```

EX16-7   10:10   03 TUE 04/06/71

```
? 100
 1.05243
? 200
 .96604
? 400
 1.06814
? 800
 .989602
? 1600
 .98862
? 3200
 1.0112
? 6400
 .996965
? 12800
 1.01132
? S
```

We know that the correct answer is 1.000. This method
of computing the area under a curve is not particularly accurate and should be used only when other methods cannot be
used.

Before we can discuss the next problem, you must understand what is meant by two-dimensional arrays. In past chapters you had occasion to write such statements as:

DIM X(50)

or

DIM A(20), B(10), C(10)

These statements reserve computer locations; 50 in the
first example, 20, 10, and 10 in the second.

Here is another way to write a DIM statement.

DIM W(5,4)

W is a two-dimensional figure or array. The array has
5 rows and 4 columns. In memory, it can be imagined as
appearing like this:

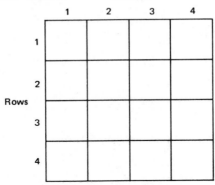

Figure 16-8

The DIM statement reserves 20 computer locations. The
two integers within parentheses represent *rows* and *columns*,
respectively.

Let's write a very simple program where we simply put
numbers into a two-dimensional array, then print them out.

140

```
10   DIM X(5,3)
20   MAT READ X
30   MAT PRINT X
40   DATA 1, 2, 3, 11, 12, 13, 21, 22, 23
50   DATA 31, 32, 33, 41, 42, 43
```

Here is the printout:

EX16-8   11:37   03 TUE 04/06/71

1	2	3
11	12	13
21	22	23
31	32	33
41	42	43

This program uses two MAT operations. MAT stands for
"matrix." In the BASIC language there are eleven MAT operations, but in this text we'll look at only MAT READ and MAT
PRINT. These are easy to understand. The example shows that
the values in the DATA statement are stored into the named
array (X) by rows. That is, the first row gets the first
three values; the second row, the next three; etc. The array
is composed of 5 rows and 3 columns; therefore, 15 values
must be found in the DATA statement to satisfy the MAT READ
instruction. The MAT PRINT instruction prints out all of the
array.

Let's try a problem involving a two-dimensional array.
Assume you have a 5 x 5 array. Load it with 25 values from
a DATA statement, then have the computer sum all 25 values.

You'll need a loop within a loop. Here's the program:
```
10   DIM A(5,5)
20   MAT READ A
```

(Continued on next page)

141

```
30   LET S = 0
40   FOR I = 1 TO 5
50   FOR J = 1 TO 5
60   LET S = S + A(I,J)
70   NEXT J
80   NEXT I
90   PRINT S
100  DATA 1, 2, 3, 4, 5, 6, 7, 8, 9, 10
110  DATA 2, 3, 4, 5, 6, 7, 8, 9, 10, 11
120  DATA 3, 4, 5, 6, 7
```

The twenty-five values of array S will be arranged rec-
tangularly in memory. You can imagine them appearing this
way:

1	2	3	4	5
6	7	8	9	10
2	3	4	5	6
7	8	9	10	11
3	4	5	6	7

Figure 16-9

At line 60 of the above program, the subscript for A is
I,J. The initial values of I and J will be 1 and 1 respectively. J varies from 1 to 5 while I remains constant at 1.
Then I changes to 2 and J varies again from 1 to 5. This
procedure repeats until I becomes 5 and J cycles from 1 to
5 for the last time.

You can see that the equation at line 60 will be executed 25 times. The values of the subscripts as the equation
is executed are these:

I	J
1	1
1	2
1	3
1	4
1	5
2	1
2	2
2	3
2	4
2	5
3	1
3	2
3	3
⋮	⋮
5	3
5	4
5	5

These subscripts will access and add to S, the values of A(row 1, column 1), A(row 1, column 2), etc., to A(row 5, column

In an earlier chapter we gave an exercise where a white knight and a black knight moved about on a chessboard until they collided. In this next problem a single knight is involved. His initial position is in the square at the upper left-hand corner of the chessboard. The problem is to have him move on the chessboard in such a way that he visits each of the 64 squares at least once. We are to write a program which causes the knight to move randomly. The program must count the number of moves he makes until the requirement that he visits all squares is fulfilled.

Study the next illustration:

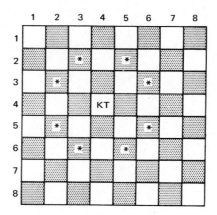

Figure 16-10

The rows are numbered from 1 to 8, inclusive as are the columns. In the illustration the knight is shown at location 4,4 (fourth row, fourth column). The asterisks show to where the knight can move from that position. The problem requires that the knight's initial position be 1,1 (first row, first column).

It's not difficult to have the knight move and to count the number of moves he makes. The difficult part of the problem is to have the program know whether or not he has visited any given square.

To overcome the difficulty, we introduce an 8 by 8 array which we'll call A. The array will initially be filled with zeroes.

	1	2	3	4	5	6	7	8
1	0	0	0	0	0	0	0	0
2	0	0	0	0	0	0	0	0
3	0	0	0	0	0	0	0	0
4	0	0	0	0	0	0	0	0
5	0	0	0	0	0	0	0	0
6	0	0	0	0	0	0	0	0
7	0	0	0	0	0	0	0	0
8	0	0	0	0	0	0	0	0

Figure 16-11

The value zero in a square means that the knight has not yet
visited that square; the value 1 means that it has.

Whenever the knight makes a legal move on the chessboard, 1 is added to a move counter. Also, to reflect the
fact that the knight has moved to a given square of the chessboard, the value in the corresponding location of the array
must be changed from zero to 1.

A flowchart which can be used to solve this problem
is shown on the next page.

The meanings of the various symbols shown in the flowchart are:

      K tells when all 64 squares have been visited.
      N counts number of legal moves made.
      R reflects position of knight on row.
      C reflects position of knight on column.

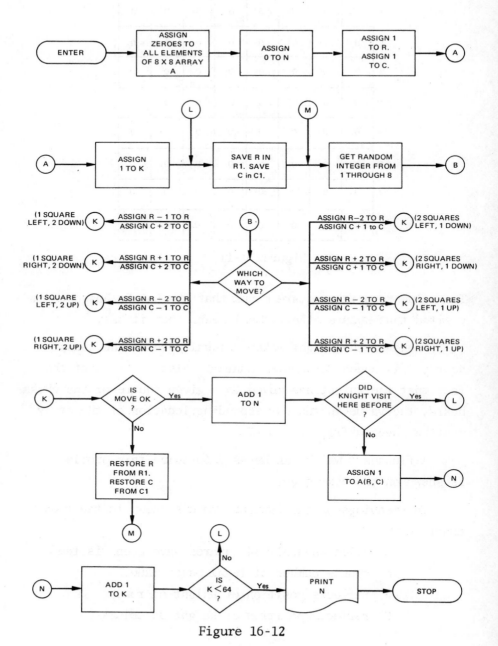

Figure 16-12

Here is the corresponding program:

```
10   DIM A(8,8)
20   FOR I = 1 TO 8
30   FOR J = 1 TO 8
40   LET A(I,J) = 0
50   NEXT J
60   NEXT I
70   LET N = 0
80   LET R = 1
90   LET C = 1
100  FOR K = 1 TO 64
110  LET R1 = R
120  LET C1 = C
130  LET Q = INT(RND(-1) * 8) + 1
140  ON Q GO TO 150,180,210,240,270,300,330,360
150  LET R = R - 2
160  LET C = C + 1
170  GO TO 380
180  LET R = R + 2
190  LET C = C + 1
200  GO TO 380
210  LET R = R - 2
220  LET C = C - 1
230  GO TO 380
240  LET R = R + 2
250  LET C = C - 1
260  GO TO 380
270  LET R = R - 1
280  LET C = C + 2
290  GO TO 380
300  LET R = R + 1
```

(Continued on next page)

```
310 LET C = C + 2
320 GO TO 380
330 LET R = R - 1
340 LET C = C - 2
350 GO TO 380
360 LET R = R + 1
370 LET C = C - 2
380 IF R < 1 THEN 460
390 IF R > 8 THEN 460
400 IF C < 1 THEN 460
410 IF C > 8 THEN 460
420 LET N = N + 1
430 IF A(R,C) = 1 THEN 110
440 LET A(R,C) = 1
450 GO TO 490
460 LET R = R1
470 LET C = C1
480 GO TO 130
490 NEXT K
500 PRINT N
510 STOP
```

Here are the results of two runs of this program:

```
EX16-9          8:29      03 FRI 04/09/71
  410


EX-10           8:29      03 FRI 04/09/71
  481
```

BASIC MINI-LESSON:

Arrays in BASIC can have either single or double dimensions.

The MAT READ command reads in from the DATA statement all the values necessary to load a two-dimensional array. The values in the DATA statement must be ordered by rows; first all the values for row 1, then all the values for row 2, etc.

The MAT PRINT command prints out the entire contents of a two-dimensional array.

EXERCISES:

1. Suppose you have a box filled with 100 slips of paper. All are blank except one which reads "success."

It is well known that if you reach into the box and pull out a slip at random, you have one chance in 100 of pulling out the slip marked "success." Assume, however, that you may have up to 100 draws, replacing blank slips in the box should you draw a blank. Now, what are the chances of drawing the magic slip?

Since failing blank slips are returned to the box after each draw, each draw has one chance in one hundred of yielding the correct one. But the chances of pulling out the "success" slip, given up to 100 draws, is much greater. Have a program simulate this game.

Only one successful draw is necessary in the game. If that successful draw is the first one, then the game is over.

Use random numbers to simulate successive draws. In the

first game did your program draw the "success" slip within the restrictions mentioned above? The answer is either "yes" or "no." So one game doesn't tell very much. Have the program play 100 games, having it keep track of how many yeses there were in those games. Now the ratio of total yeses to total games played is meaningful. It approximates the chances of drawing the "success" slip in any one game.

There is a simple equation involving "e" (2.71828....) which gives the answer to this problem directly. From your simulation results see if you can determine what this equation must be.

2. Mathematicians claim that in a random group of about 22 or 23 people, the chances are about 1 in 2 that two or more of the people will have the same birthday (month and day only).

Write a program to select no more than 23 birthdays at random and have the program check whether any two of them are identical. Run the program several times.

3. We know a brilliant young author who recently wrote a great novel. He hit upon a plan for submitting it to prospective publishers. He garnered a list of several hundred publishers' names and resolved to send a copy of his book *each day* to a different publisher.

He sent along enough postage so that if a publisher rejected his text, the publisher could return it to him. The author also resolved to send out all returned manuscripts, as soon as he received them, in addition to the regular one-a-day disbursements. (Obviously, the author needed many copies of his novel, but he had a copying machine at his disposal.)

It is well known that publishers return rejected texts within 5 to 21 days of their receipt. For this problem, assume time spent in return transit is negligible and that the author can expect to receive back submitted manuscripts anywhere from 5 to 21 days after he sends them out.

The problem is to predict how many manuscripts the author will receive back each day from the 6th thru the 79th day of his campaign. (The author received an acceptance on the 80th day).

Use random numbers to solve the problem. Run the program several times so that you can get a good representation of what is likely to happen on the various days.

Your solution should show that at first (up to about the 15th day), only a few manuscripts will be received back. Subsequently, returns begin to build up. After about the 35th day, seldom will a day go by without a return. Later the author can expect to receive as many as ten or twelve manuscripts in one day.

In order to solve this problem your program will have to generate random integers from 5 through 21. You can use this BASIC statement:

    LET R = INT(RND(-1) * 17) + 5

You can make this program slightly more difficult by showing the return of the remaining manuscripts outstanding, from day 80 thru 100. No additional manuscripts are submitted to publishers during this period, of course.

4.   Consider an inclined grid which looks like this:

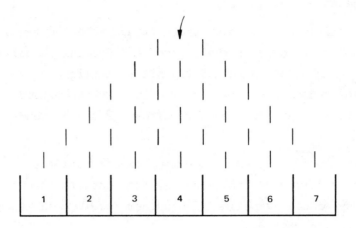

Drop a ball into the opening indicated by the arrow. Have the ball roll down the incline randomly, selecting a path as it rolls into one of the pockets numbered 1 thru 7.

Repeat the procedure several times, then count the number of balls in each of the pockets. You'll find most of the balls are congregated in pockets 3, 4 and 5. A fewer number of balls are found in pockets 1,2,6 and 7. This is what you'd expect.

Simulate the shape of a "normal curve" by expanding to 41 the number of pockets in the bottom row. Expand also, as required, the structure above that bottom row. Now, drop 1000 balls through the opening at the top of the structure.

Have the computer simulate the dropping of 1000 balls, have it count the number of balls rolling into each pocket of the bottom row, then have it print the results.

Chapter 17

SORTING

   In solving problems it is often necessary to place a
series of numbers in ascending or descending sequence. In
this chapter we will examine various ways that this task can
be accomplished. To permit comparison of the various methods
we will use the same sequence of unsorted numbers. That sequence is:

10	6	8	3	12	15	3	1	7	11	8

   There are only eleven numbers in this sequence (note
that there are two 3's and two 8's), but any scheme that
will work for eleven numbers will work for any number of numbers.

   In all the examples which follow, the sort sequence desired will be ascending. Of course the same principles
would apply if the sequence desired were descending.

   The first method we'll explore is a "brute force" approach. We place the numbers in a list (call it A) like
the one shown on page 154.

   Then we'll have the program search the list to find the
smallest value and place that value at the head of another
list (call it B) having the same size as A. That smallest
value in A is then changed to a very large value, say 99999.

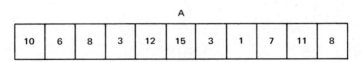

A

| 10 | 6 | 8 | 3 | 12 | 15 | 3 | 1 | 7 | 11 | 8 |

Figure 17-1

This is the appearance of lists A and B after the program has found the smallest value in list A and that value has been changed to 99999.

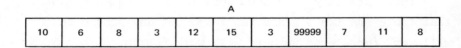

A

| 10 | 6 | 8 | 3 | 12 | 15 | 3 | 99999 | 7 | 11 | 8 |

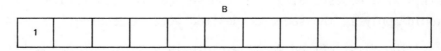

B

| 1 | | | | | | | | | | |

Figure 17-2

The next step is to again find the smallest value in list A, place that value in the second position of list B and replace the smallest in list A with 99999.

154

This is the appearance of lists A and B after the program has found the second smallest value in list A and that value has been changed to 99999.

A

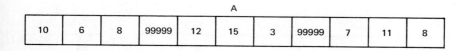

| 10 | 6 | 8 | 99999 | 12 | 15 | 3 | 99999 | 7 | 11 | 8 |

B

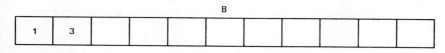

| 1 | 3 | | | | | | | | | |

Figure 17-3

You've seen that there are two 3's in list A. The program finds the *first* one to be the smallest. You'll probably also realize that the value 99999 must be carefully chosen. The user must know, without a doubt, that this value is larger than any of the original values in list A.

The program continues using this procedure, searching list A for the smallest value time and time again. Since there are eleven values in list A, the program will have to search the list eleven times. After the *tenth* search has been completed, the appearance of the two lists is as shown in Figure 17-4 on page 156.

When the program searches through the A list for the eleventh time, the smallest value it finds is 15. This value is placed at the bottom of list B, 99999 is placed in the sixth position of the A list and the task is complete. List B will then contain the sorted values.

155

					A					
99999	99999	99999	99999	99999	15	99999	99999	99999	99999	99999

				B					
1	3	3	6	7	8	8	10	11	12

Figure 17-4

The flowchart shows how the program could be written:

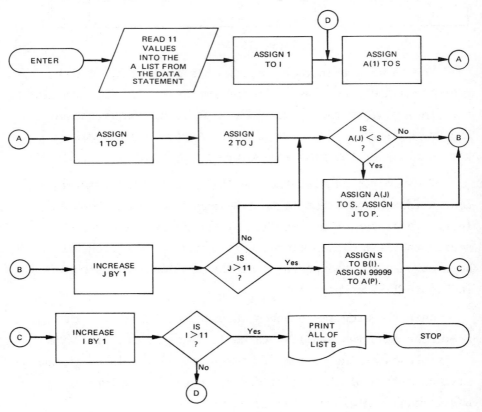

Figure 17-5

156

In the flowchart, I controls the number of times list A will be searched. It varies from 1 through 11. I also acts as a subscript assigning S, the smallest value found by each search, to list B.

At the beginning of each search the program assigns the *first* value of list A to S, then checks the remainder of the list to determine whether another value is smaller than S. Whenever a value smaller than S is found, it replaces S. Each search examines values 2 through 11 only of list A because the first value has already been assigned to S. J controls the values being looked at during any one search through the A list. P contains the position of the smallest value. During any of the eleven searches, its initial value is 1, but when S changes, P must change. The value assigned to P when S changes is J because at all times J holds the position of the A value being compared with S.

At the end of each search, S contains the smallest value found during the search and P contains its position in the A list. The value of P is needed so that 99999 can be assigned to the place in the A list holding the smallest number. After 99999 has been assigned to that position, the A list has been prepared for the next search.

The BASIC coding for this problem is given as an assignment under the exercises for this chapter.

A better way to sort is the "interchange" method. Take the original unsorted values and store them in list A.

Now have the program examine the first two values of list A. Are they already in sequence? If so, leave them alone; if not interchange the values.

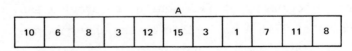

Figure 17-6

In the example, the first two values are 10 and 6. They are not in sequence. Therefore, the two values are inter-changed. List A now looks like this:

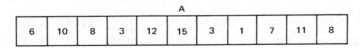

Figure 17-7

Now have the program examine the values in the second and third positions of list A. Are they in sequence? If so, leave them alone. If not, interchange them. The values are 10 and 8. They must be interchanged.

The next examination involves values 10 and 3. They are

158

not in sequence and must therefore be interchanged.

The next examination involves values 10 and 12. They are in sequence and no action is taken. Values 12 and 15 are also in sequence. However, the values 15 and 3 will cause another "swap."

This procedure continues until list A has been processed once. At that time its appearance is this:

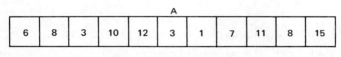

Figure 17-8

There are eleven values in the list but only 10 *pairs* of values. All ten pairs have been examined with the end result that the *largest value has fallen to the bottom of the list*. We must now process the list again.

Since we know that the largest value is at the bottom of the list, we need to examine only 9 pairs of values during the second pass through the list.

Again we examine the values in pairs. Whenever two values are in sequence, we leave them alone; whenever they're not, we interchange them. Here is the result of the second pass through list A:

159

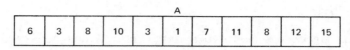

Figure 17-9

This pass has examined only 9 pairs of values in list A, and has forced the second largest value to the second position from the bottom.

You can see that 10 passes through list A are needed to sort 11 values. The first pass looks at 10 pairs of values; the second, 9; the third, 8; etc. The last pass through list A involves the program's looking at the first and second value of the list (a single pair).

Here is the appearance of list A *just before* the tenth pass is made:

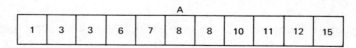

Figure 17-10

160

The list is in sequence. No interchange is needed and the list may now be printed out.

It can be seen that the list may be completely sequenced *before* the final pass is made. The program can be written to test whether its execution can be terminated ahead of schedule. In the flowchart which follows, F tells whether the passes can be terminated ahead of time.

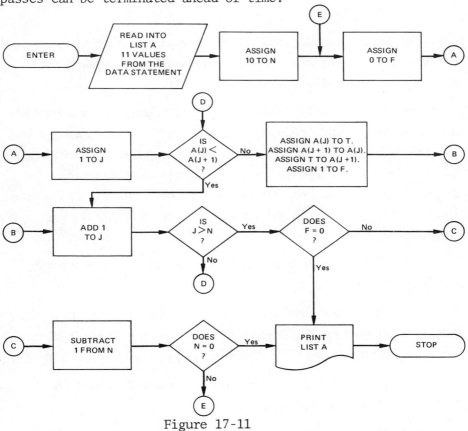

Figure 17-11

There are several important points to be observed in this flowchart. First subscripts may be computed. In other words, an expression such as J + 1 or (X + Y)/Z may be placed within parentheses following the name of a list. That

161

value of the expression will be the subscript. It's OK therefore, to write a BASIC IF statement like this:

    50 IF A(J) < A (J + 1) THEN 80

Next, observe how the interchange is made. It would not be logical to do this:

    60 LET A(J) = A(J + 1)
    70 LET A(J + 1) = A(J)

The values in A(J) and A(J + 1) would then be identical. A temporary holding cell, T, is used to save the value of A(J) *before* A(J + 1) is assigned to A(J).

The value F checks whether *any* interchange of values has occurred during any one pass through list A. If F remains at its initial setting of zero, no interchange has occurred and the job is done. If even *one* interchange has occurred, F is set to 1 and another pass will be required (unless, of course the interchange took place during the last scheduled pass through the list).

The coding for this program will be assigned under the exercises for this chapter.

A still better way to sort values in a list is the Shell Method developed by Dr. Donald L. Shell of the General Electric Company, Research & Development Laboratory, Schenectady, N.Y.

To begin, let's place the eleven unsorted values in list A as shown in Figure 17-12.

Have the program compare the value in position 1 of the list with the value in position 6, the exact mid-point of the list. If the values are in sequence, leave them alone; if not interchange them.

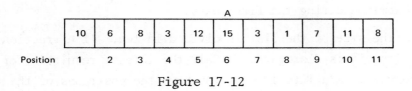

Figure 17-12

In the example, the two values are 10 and 15. They are in sequence, so no action is taken. Now have the program examine the second and seventh values. These are not in sequence so a swap is made. After the interchange has taken place, list A looks like this:

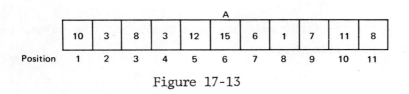

Figure 17-13

In like manner, the program examines the values at positions 3 and 8, 4 and 9, 5 and 10, 6 and 11. As always, when the two values are in sequence, no action takes place;

163

when the values are not in sequence, they are interchanged. The program has made the *first* pass through list A, but more passes are necessary.

Let's determine the rules which govern what values will be examined during the first pass.

The size of the list is divided in two. If a fraction results, it is disregarded. Call the integer result I (for interval). Add I to 1. Now you have the positions of the two values to examine. They are:

       1 and I + 1
       2 and I + 2
       3 and I + 3
              etc.

Where the size of the list is 11, I is 5 and the values to examine are located at the positions

       1 and 6
       2 and 7
       3 and 8
       4 and 9
       5 and 10
       6 and 11

After the first pass has been completed, the values in list A look like this:

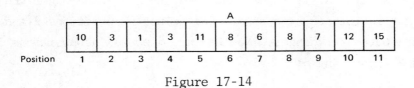

A										
10	3	1	3	11	8	6	8	7	12	15

Position   1   2   3   4   5   6   7   8   9   10   11

Figure 17-14

To prepare for the second pass, the size of the list is divided by 4. The result becomes I. As before, disregard fractions.) I is then added to 1. The positions of the values to be examined are now determined by

1 and I + 1
2 and I + 2
3 and I + 3
      etc.

Where the size of the list is 11, the values to examine are at positions

1 and 3
2 and 4
3 and 5
4 and 6
5 and 7
6 and 8
7 and 9
8 and 10
9 and 11

165

Note that I must be 2 when 11 is divided by 4. Only the integer portion of the result is used.

When your program examines the values at position 1 and 3 of the list A, it finds that they are not in sequence and therefore interchanges them. The values at positions 2 and 4 are not interchanged. Neither are the ones at positions 3 and 5, and 4 and 6.

The values at positions 5 and 7 must be interchanged. At this point, list A looks like this:

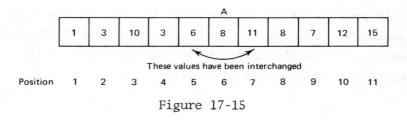

Figure 17-15

Now, instead of going forward to examine the values located at positions 6 and 8, the program *backs up* to *recheck* positions 3 and 5. The swap of values located at positions 3 and 7 *triggered* the recheck of the previously examined values.

Observe that the values at positions 3 and 5 are not in sequence and are, therefore, interchanged. If they had been in sequence, an interchange would not have taken place and no further back up would have been needed. In the example, the interchange of values located at positions 3 and 5

166

causes another back up to positions 1 and 3. No interchange of the values located at positions 1 and 3 is necessary.

The program keeps backing up until it can no longer do so or until the comparison of two values in the list *does not* trigger an interchange.

In the present example, list A now looks like this:

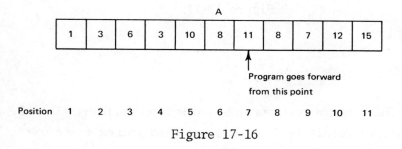

Figure 17-16

Now the program continues from the point where the forward movement was interupted. The forward movement was interupted by the interchange of values located at positions 5 and 7. The program now looks at values located at positions 6 and 8. No interchange is needed. However, the values at positions 7 and 9 are not in sequence. They're interchanged. This triggers an examination and interchange of values located at positions 5 and 7. The subsequent examination of the values in positions 3 and 5 shows that no further backing up is needed. Forward motion through list A resumes. The program looks at the values in positions 8 and 10. and 9 and 11 and finds that they are OK. List A now looks like this:

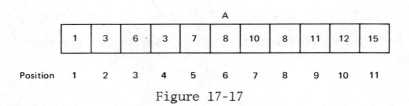

	A									
1	3	6	3	7	8	10	8	11	12	15

Position   1   2   3   4   5   6   7   8   9   10   11

Figure 17-17

The program now computes a new I by dividing 11 by 8. The integer result is 1. Therefore, the values to be examined are:

1 and 2
2 and 3
3 and 4
4 and 5
5 and 6
6 and 7
7 and 8
8 and 9
9 and 10
10 and 11

When I is 1, backing up is necessary as it was when I was 2. In this example when I was 5, backing up was impossible except for one special situation. Can you see why?

When this third pass has been made, I is again computed and found to be zero. The program stops when I is zero since

168

the job is done. The 11 values in the A list must now be in sequence.

You can see that the Shell method of sorting requires that the size of the list be divided first by 2, then by 4, then 8, etc.

When all values to be sorted can be stored in a single list, this method provides the fastest way to sort. Here is a flowchart showing the Shell Method:

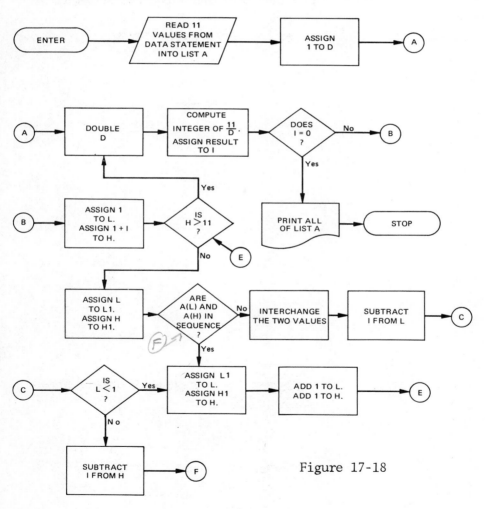

Figure 17-18

169

EXERCISES:

1. Write the BASIC coding which agrees with the "brute force" method of sorting.

2. Write the BASIC coding which agrees with the "inter-change" method of sorting.

3. Write the BASIC coding which agrees with the Shell Method of sorting. Since I looks so much like 1, use J in your program wherever the flowchart shows I.

Chapter 18

TAPE SORTING

The previous chapter showed how to sort efficiently when all the numbers involved could be held in the memory of the computer.

There are occasions when the numbers to be sorted cannot all be stored at one time in the memory of the computer. Under those circumstances, *portions* of the numbers are sorted, then *other portions*, then finally all sorted portions are merged.

Consider an artificial example where 20 unsorted numbers located on a reel of magnetic tape (tape A) are to be sorted and sequenced in ascending order. These are the numbers:

13, 16, 12, 18, 6, 8, 112, 7, 6, 3, 19, 11, 5, 4, 1, 15, 4, 11, 9, 5

The numbers are brought into memory and transferred to two additional reels of tape (Tapes B and C). Tape B gets the first, third, fifth, etc., numbers of the original list and Tape C gets the second, fourth, sixth, etc., numbers of the original list. The latter two tapes now look like this:

```
TAPE B   13  12  6  112  6  19  5   1   4  9
TAPE C   16  18  8    7  3  11  4  15  11  5
```

The next step is to merge the numbers on these two tapes

171

back to the first tape (Tape A). Doing this erases the numbers which were originally stored on that tape. We have the computer read into memory a value from tape B and a value from Tape C. Those values are shown below:

MEMORY

FROM TAPE B	FROM TAPE C
13	16

Since 13 is less than 16, the program transfers the value 13 to Tape A, then reads another value from Tape B. Memory now looks like this:

MEMORY

FROM TAPE B	FROM TAPE C
12	16

Since 12 is less than 16, the program transfers the value 12 to Tape A, then reads another value from Tape B:

MEMORY

FROM TAPE B	FROM TAPE C
6	16

Again, the value 6 is recorded on Tape A and the program reads the next value from Tape B:

MEMORY

FROM TAPE B	FROM TAPE C
112	16

172

This time the value 16 is recorded on Tape A and the program reads the next value from Tape C.

MEMORY

FROM TAPE B	FROM TAPE C
112	18

The value 18 is less than 112, therefore, 18 is recorded on Tape A. A glance at the contents of Tape C will show you that all the remaining values of Tape C are less than 112. Therefore, all those values are recorded on Tape A.

When either of the tapes is exhausted, the remaining values from the other tape are recorded on Tape A.

Tape A now looks like this:

13 12 6 16 18 8 7 3 11 4 15 11 5 112 6 19 5 1 4 9

The next step is simply to repeat the procedure. Break up tape A into two tapes, then merge them back into Tape A. This is the breakout:

TAPE B   13   6   18   7   11   15   5   6   5   4

TAPE C   12   16   8   3   4   11   112   19   1   9

And this is the result of the merger back to tape A.

TAPE A

12 13 6 16 8 3 4 11 18 7 11 15 5 6 5 4 112 19 1 9

Another breakout:

TAPE B   12   6   8   4   18   11   5   5   112   1

TAPE C   13   16   3   11   7   15   6   4   19   9

And another merge:

173

12 6 8 4 13 16 3 11 7 15 6 4 18 11 5 5 19 9 112 1

This process continues several more times until the job is complete. Here are the contents of Tape A as it existed originally, and as it looked at the end of each merge.

13	16	12	18	6	8	112	7	6	3	19
11	5	4	1	15	4	11	9	5		

13	12	6	16	18	8	7	3	11	4	15
11	5	112	6	19	5	1	4	9		

12	13	6	16	8	3	4	11	18	7	11
15	5	6	5	4	112	19	1	9		

12	6	8	4	13	16	3	11	7	15	6
4	18	11	5	5	19	9	112	1		

6	4	12	8	13	3	7	6	16	11	15
4	11	5	9	1	18	5	19	112		

4	6	8	3	6	11	4	5	1	5	12
13	7	16	15	11	9	18	19	112		

4	6	3	8	6	4	1	11	5	5	12
7	13	15	9	16	11	18	19	112		

4	3	6	6	1	5	8	4	11	5	7
12	13	9	11	15	16	18	19	112		

3	4	6	5	4	5	6	1	8	11	7
12	9	13	11	15	16	18	19	112		

3	4	5	5	1	6	4	6	8	7	9
11	11	12	13	15	16	18	19	112		

3	4	5	5	1	4	6	6	7	8	9
11	11	12	13	15	16	18	19	112		

3	4	5	4	5	1	6	6	7	8	9
11	11	12	13	15	16	18	19	112		

3	4	4	1	5	5	6	6	7	8	9
11	11	12	13	15	16	18	19	112		

3	4	1	4	5	5	6	6	7	8	9
11	11	12	13	15	16	18	19	112		

3	1	4	4	5	5	6	6	7	8	9
11	11	12	13	15	16	18	19	112		

1	3	4	4	5	5	6	6	7	8	9
11	11	12	13	15	16	18	19	112		

You can see that each break out of Tape A and each merge back to Tape A improves the order of the numbers. The last merge, of course, shows the numbers sorted in increasing sequence.

This sorting method is very inefficient. Many other methods exist which either involve more than three tapes or more sophisticated sorting techniques, or both.*

EXERCISE:

1. Write a flowchart and program which simulates the tape sort method described in this chapter. Have the program read twenty values from a DATA statement into list A. (This list simulates Tape A.) Then have the program break out list A into lists B and C. (These lists simulate Tapes B and C.)

    Your program must print the original values in list A and also the contents of list A after every merge. The program must also determine when to stop. (An easy way to do this, is to have the program check the sequence of the numbers in list A after every merge. If the numbers are in sequence, the job is done; if not, another breakout and merge is required.)

    Have the program print JOB COMPLETE when the task has been successfully accomplished.

---

* The person faced with an actual sorting problem should obtain a copy of Computer Sorting by Ivan Flores, Prentice-Hall, Inc., Englewood Cliffs, New Jersey 07632.

Chapter 19

ALPHANUMERIC MANIPULATIONS

In the last few lessons you dealt with random numbers,
loops, subscripts, searching and sorting. This chapter pre-
sents a change of pace. Instead of dealing with numeric
values, we will deal with alphabetic as well as numeric data.

Let's begin by running this simple program:

```
10   LET A$ = "HELLO "
20   READ B$
30   PRINT A$;B$
40   DATA THERE
RUN
```

The output from the program is this:

```
EX19-1              10:47           03 MON 04/12/71

HELLO THERE
```

You can see that the value HELLO is assigned to A$ and
the value THERE is assigned to B$. Now observe these impor-
tant points:

1.   You can assign an alphanumeric value to a data name
     by writing a statement such as the one in line 10.
     Note the quotation marks around the value.

2.   Data names which hold alphanumeric values end with
     a dollar sign. The usual rules for forming data

176

names apply except that a name may only be a *single letter followed by a dollar sign.*

3. Alphanumeric values may be shown in DATA statements.

Alphanumeric data items are called *strings*. Strings may be up to 15 characters in length (on some time-sharing systems, strings may be longer than 15 characters) and may include blanks. If an item in a DATA statement begins with a digit or has an imbedded comma, it must be enclosed with quotation marks. Note this example:

```
10   READ A$, B$, C$
20   PRINT A$; B$; C$
30   DATA JULY, " 25,", " 1970"
```

The value JULY is assigned to A$; the value   25,   is assigned to B$; the value   1970   is assigned to C$.

When you type RUN, the printout is this:

EX19-2   10:48   03 MON 04/12/71

JULY 25, 1970

You can test one alphanumeric value against another. For instance, you may write:

```
25   IF A$ = "END" THEN 45
```

or
```
60   IF A$ > B$ THEN 80
```

When comparing one alphanumeric value against another, you should understand the "official" sequence of characters: digits precede letters. Letters increase in sequence from A through Z. A chart later in this lesson shows the relative positions of letters, digits, and special characters.

177

You may set up alphanumeric arrays. Do it this way:

    10   DIM X$(50), Y$(20),Z$(200)

Now let's solve some problems. Suppose we need a program which will accept words from the teletype and define them. Here is a flowchart which shows how the program may be written:

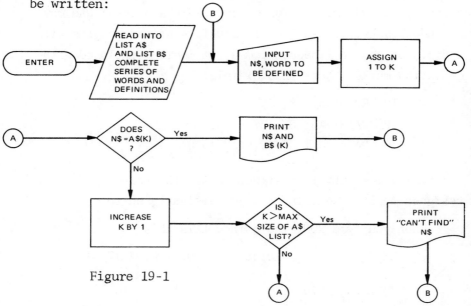

Figure 19-1

Let's reserve for lists A$ and B$ ten locations each. We're not asking a great deal from this program. It defines only 10 words; but if it works for 10, it ought to work for a thousand.

Here's the BASIC program and a sample run: (Note that the word DATA in lines 500, 510, 520, 530, and 540 is not part of the data items themselves.)

    5   DIM A$(10), B$(10)
    10   FOR I = 1 TO 10
    20   READ A$(I), B$(I)

(Continued on next page)

178

```
 30  NEXT I
 40  INPUT N$
 50  FOR K = 1 TO 10
 60  IF A$(K) = N$ THEN 100
 70  NEXT K
 80  PRINT "CAN'T FIND "; N$
 90  GO TO 40
100  PRINT A$(K), B$(K)
110  GO TO 40
500  DATA SALES TAX, TAX ON GOODS, SOAP
510  DATA CLEANSING AGENT, PENCIL, WRITING DEVICE
520  DATA DICTIONARY, LIST OF WORDS, WOMAN
530  DATA KIND OF HUMAN, BASIC, ELEMENTARY, LANGUAGE
540  DATA SPEECH MEDIUM, FILCH, STEAL FURTIVELY
550  DATA PROGRAM, INSTRUCTIONS, COMPUTER, CALCULATOR
RUN
```

EX19-3   10:56   03 MON 04/12/71

```
? WOMAN
WOMAN           KIND OF HUMAN
? COMPUTER
COMPUTER        CALCULATOR
? BUILDING
CAN'T FIND BUILDING
? FILCH
FILCH           STEAL FURTIVELY
?
```

The program is stopped manually when you have all the definitions you want. Arrays A$ and B$ are not really needed in this program. Note below how we can read alphanumeric values from the DATA statement and examine them without

179

storing them in arrays: (Data is not shown.)

```
 10  INPUT N$
 20  FOR K = 1 TO 10
 30  READ A$, B$
 40  IF A$ = N$ THEN 90
 50  NEXT K
 60  PRINT "CAN'T FIND" ; N$
 70  RESTORE
 80  GO TO 10
 90  PRINT A$, B$
100  GO TO 70
```

RESTORE is a useful BASIC instruction. It directs the computer to permit reading data again from the beginning. That data may be either alphanumeric or numeric.

Let's try a simple language-translating program for our next problem. Again, we're not trying to be too sophisticated; we're translating in the simplest way possible: by entering a foreign word and getting its English equivalent.

You'll see that this program is virtually identical to the word definitions program above. Because of this, a flow-chart is not needed.

The language being translated is German.

```
 10  RESTORE
 20  INPUT N$
 30  FOR L = 1 TO 11
 40  READ A$, B$
 50  IF A$ = N$ THEN 90
 60  NEXT L
 70  PRINT "XXXXX"
 80  GO TO 10
```

(Continued on next page)

```
90   PRINT B$
100  GO TO 10
110  DATA HEIR, HERE, DA, THERE, JUNG, "YOUNG"
120  DATA IST, IS, MANN, MAN, SCHULER, "STUDENT"
130  DATA DER, THE, KNABE, BOY, LEHRER, "TEACHER"
140  DATA UND, AND, ALT, "OLD"
```

Quotation marks around the words YOUNG, STUDENT, TEACHER and OLD, in this example, are optional. You'll recall that you *must* place quotation marks around alphanumeric data values only when they begin with a digit or include an imbedded comma.

When you type RUN, you may request output similar to this:

```
EX19-4        17:20        03 MON 04/19/71

? HEIR
HERE
? DER
THE
? DA
THERE
? KNABE
BOY
? OLD
XXXXX
? JUNG
YOUNG
? S
```

181

Observe that when an English word cannot be found, the program prints XXXXX.

With this next problem, we're going to make cryptographers of you. Suppose it is necessary for you to transmit this message:

MEET ME TONIGHT AT SIX SHARP

Can you write a program which will convert this message to a meaningless jumble of characters which only your correspondent can unravel?

The first thing we must do is change the message a bit (include hyphens between words):

MEET-ME-TONIGHT-AT-SIX-SHARP

Now, let's call up a series of random numbers to scramble the message. Examine this flowchart:

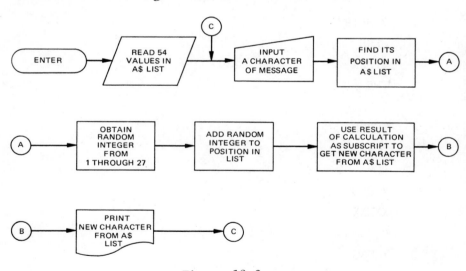

Figure 19-2

These are the 54 values to store in the A$ list:
ABCDEFGHIJKLMNOPQRSTUVWXYZ-ABCDEFGHIJKLMNOPQRSTUVWXYZ-

As you can see, the list consists of 26 letters of the alphabet, a hyphen, 26 more letters and a final hyphen. There are, therefore, two halves to the list, the left and the right.

If we have the program search for a character, the computer will find it in the left-hand portion of the list. The computer can then note its position in that list. For instance, the letter M is in position 13, the hyphen is in position 27 of the list.

Now an integer selected at random from 1 to 27, when added to a character's A$ position, will give a new integer which can be used as a subscript enabling the computer to select another value from the list.

Let's take the first few characters of the message:

M	E	E	T	-	M	E	MESSAGE CHARACTERS
13	5	5	20	27	13	5	LIST POSITIONS
20	9	5	3	2	6	21	RANDOM INTEGERS
33	14	10	23	29	19	26	CALCULATED POSITIONS OF NEW CHARACTERS IN A$ LIST
F	N	J	W	B	S	Z	NEW CHARACTERS

The new message uses characters from both the left and right-hand positions of the A$ list. To decode the message, your correspondent must reverse the procedure. Naturally, he has to have access to the *same series of random integers* that you had. Fortunately, we may easily instruct the computer to repeat the same sequence of random numbers over and over again.

Study this program:

```
5    DIM A$(54)
10   FOR I = 1 TO 54
20   READ A$(I)
30   NEXT I
40   INPUT M$
50   FOR K = 1 TO 27
60   IF A$(K) = M$ THEN 100
70   NEXT K
80   PRINT "ERROR IN DATA"
90   GO TO 40
100  LET S = INT(RND(0) * 27) + 1
110  PRINT A$(S + K)
120  GO TO 40
130  DATA A, B, C, D, E, F, G, H, I, J, K, L, M
140  DATA N, O, P, Q, R, S, T, U, V, W, X, Y, Z
150  DATA -
160  DATA A, B, C, D, E, F, G, H, I, J, K, L, M
170  DATA N, O, P, W, R, S, T, U, V, Q, X, Y, Z
180  DATA -
```

Here's the program in execution:

```
EX19-5              11:23           03 FRI 04/09/71
? M
F
? E
N
? E
J
? T
W
? -
B              (Continued on next page)
```

184

```
? M
S
? E
Z
?
```

The statement at line 100 generates a random integer from 1 to 27. You've had the occasion to generate random digits within a specified span before, so this statement should not be strange to you.

In that statement, RND(0) begins a random series which is always the same. The fact that we're using RND(0) permits our correspondent to decode the message. He types the coded message as input to the same program. There is only one change which must be made when the program is used to decode a message. The data is stored in reverse order:

-ZYXWVUTSRQPONMLKJIHGFEDCBA-ZYXWVUTSRQPONMLKJIHGFEDCBA

Assuming the first part of our incoded message is this: FNJWBSZ, the program will decode it like this:

F	N	J	W	B	S	Z	MESSAGE
22	14	18	5	26	9	2	A$ LIST POSITIONS
20	9	5	3	2	6	21	RANDOM INTEGERS
42	23	23	8	28	15	23	CALCULATED CHARACTER POSITION IN A$ LIST
M	E	E	T	-	M	E	ORIGINAL MESSAGE

Caution: when you want to encode the letter S, you must enclose it within quotation marks. Otherwise, that letter will be interpreted as a signal to *stop* the program.

The program can be improved by changing INPUT M$ to READ M$ and by putting the message in a DATA statement. The program and its output would now appear like this:

```
5    DIM A$(54)
10   FOR I = 1 TO 54
20   READ A$(I)
30   NEXT I
40   READ M$
50   FOR K = 1 TO 27
60   IF A$(K) = M$ THEN 100
70   NEXT K
80   PRINT "ERROR IN DATA ";M$
90   GO TO 40
100  LET S = INT(RND(0) * 27) + 1
110  PRINT A$(S +K);
120  GO TO 40
130  DATA A, B, C, D, E, F, G, H, I, J, K, L, M
140  DATA N, O, P, Q, R, S, T, U, V, W, X, Y, Z
150  DATA -
160  DATA A, B, C, D, E, F, G, H, I, J, K, L, M
170  DATA N, O, P, Q, R, S, T, U, V, W, X, Y, Z
180  DATA -
1000 DATA M,E,E,T,-,M,E,-,T,O,N,I,G,H,T,-,A,T,-
1010 DATA S,I,X,-,S,H,A,R,P
RUN
```

EX19-6   11:31   03 FRI 04/09/71

FNJWBSZBIMJOFN-IBQRYWOXHMJJV
OUT OF DATA IN 40

Decoding the message, we use the same program with different DATA statements:

```
5    DIM A$(54)
10   FOR I = 1 TO 54
```

(Continued on next page)

186

```
20   READ A$(I)
30   NEXT I
40   READ M$
50   FOR K = 1 TO 27
60   IF A$(K) = M$ THEN 100
70   NEXT K
80   PRINT "ERROR IN DATA ";M$
90   GO TO 40
100 LET S = INT(RND(0) * 27) + 1
110 PRINT A$(S + K)
120 GO TO 40
130 DATA -
140 DATA Z,Y,X,W,V,U,T,S,R,Q,P,O,N
150 DATA M,L,K,J,I,H,G,F,E,D,C,B,A
160 DATA -
170 DATA Z,Y,X,W,V,U,T,S,R,Q,P,O,N
180 DATA M,L,K,J,I,H,G,F,E,D,C,B,A
1000 DATA F,N,J,W,B,S,Z,B,I,M,J,O,F,N,-
1010 DATA I,B,Q,R,Y,W,O,X,H,M,J,J,V
RUN
```

The result of the run:

```
EX19-7              11:40         03  FRI  04/09/71
```

```
MEET-ME-TONIGHT-AT-SIX-SHARP
OUT OF DATA IN 40
```

Be careful to supply the data correctly. A character in lines 1000 or 1010 which does not appear in the A$ table can throw everything off.

This program may be criticized on the grounds that the random number series is always the same and it may be accidentally discovered by an unauthorized person.

To overcome this disadvantage you may insert these statements at the beginning of your program:

```
1  INPUT Q
2  FOR I = 1 TO Q
3  LET X = RND(0)
4  NEXT I
```

This brief procedure "throws away" Q random numbers before the main portion of the program is run. Q may be changed frequently but, of course, you and your correspondent always know what Q is on any given day. Q can be computed on some arbitrary basis. For instance, if today's date is December 23, then Q could be 1223. If today's date is March 6, Q could be 0306 (or 306, which is equivalent.)

If you run the program and it doesn't work, possibly the message was encoded yesterday or the day before. Subtract one or two from Q and try again.

A question naturally arises regarding the "official" sequence of the characters used in programming. This sequence is not standard and varies from computer to computer. To find the sequence in the system used in this text, we placed most of the symbols used in BASIC in a data statement and had a program sort them using the Shell Method. Here is the program and the result of the run:

```
100 DATA " "
110 DATA "1","2","3","4","5","6","7","8","9","0"
120 DATA A,B,C,D,E,F,G,H,I,J,K,L,M,N,O,P,Q,R,S,T
130 DATA U,V,W,X,Y,Z
140 DATA "#","$","'","(",")","*","=","-",":"
150 DATA "↑","<",">","+","/","?"
160 DATA ";",",",",","."
```

(Continued on next page)

```
170 DIM A$(55)
180 INPUT N
190 FOR I = 1 TO N
200 READ A$(I)
210 PRINT A$(I);
220 NEXT I
230 PRINT
240 LET D = 1
250 LET D = D * 2
260 LET J = INT(N/D)
270 IF J = 0 THEN 460
280 LET L = 1
290 LET H = I + J
300 IF H > N THEN 250
310 LET L1 = L
320 LET H1 = H
330 IF A$(H) > = A$(L) THEN 410
340 LET T$ = A$(L)
350 LET A$(L) = A$(H)
360 LET A$(H) = T$
370 LET L = L - J
380 IF L < 1 THEN 410
390 LET H = H - J
400 GO TO 330
410 LET L = L1
420 LET H = H1
430 LET L = L + 1
440 LET H = H + 1
450 GO TO 300
460 FOR I = 1 TO N
470 PRINT A$(I);
```

(Continued on next page)

```
480 NEXT I
490 PRINT
RUN
```

EX19-8   11:33   03 MON 04/12/71

? 55

1234567890ABCDEFGHIJKLMNOPQRSTUVWXYZ#$'()*=-:↑<>+/?;,.
0123456789':(;=#+ABCDEFGHI.?<-JKLMNOPQR$*>↑ /STUVWXYZ,)

This program reads 55 characters into list A$ and prints them out in the order read. (Note the space in line 100 and also below the question mark in the printout.) Then the program sorts the characters and prints them in sorted sequence.

The sorted printout shows that digits precede letters of the alphabet, but that a space (blank character) is larger than R but smaller than S. The printout also shows that various characters such as *colon, asterisk, period,* and *comma* are intermingled with letters of the alphabet.

****

BASIC MINI-LESSON :

Alphanumeric information containing up to 15 characters may be assigned to variables.

Variable names for variables intended to hold alphanumeric information are formed according to the usual rules except that a dollar sign must be appended to each name.

Alphanumeric data may be shown in DATA statements. Data items are separated by commas. Quotation marks around alphanumeric data items may be optional but they must always be used when the data items begin with a digit or contains an imbedded comma.

Alphanumeric lists may be defined and used.

IF statements may be used to test alphanumeric data items. This is the official sequence of characters in BASIC:

0123456789':(;=#+ABCDEFGHI.?<-JKLMNOPQR$*>↑*space*/STUVWXYZ,)

EXERCISES:

1. Write a program which accepts, from the keyboard, a word chosen from the set of words: ZERO, ONE, TWO, THREE, FOUR, FIVE, SIX, SEVEN, EIGHT, NINE and prints the corresponding digit in numeric form. Have the program repeat this procedure until the user types the word FINIS.

2. Write a program which accepts, from the keyboard, a word ADD, SUBTRACT, MULTIPLY or DIVIDE, and two numeric values. Example:

    ADD,4.7,8.3

    Have the program perform the indicated arithmetic operation upon the two values. That is, add first to second, subtract second from first, multiply first times second, divide first by second. Then have the program repeat the procedure until the user types DONE,0,0.

3. This is a challenge problem for persons experienced with assembly-language programming. The following program (which is actual data for a BASIC program) solves a problem in assembly language. See if you can determine what is the problem being solved and how the BASIC program must be written.

    5010 DATA DEF, 0, VALUE OF ZERO
    5020 DATA DEF, 2, VALUE OF TWO
    5030 DATA DEF, 3.1416, VALUE OF PI

    (Continued on next page)

191

```
5040 DATA DEF, 0, VALUE OF R
5050 DATA DEF, 0, VALUE OF C
5060 DATA RED, 4, READ VALUE OF R
5070 DATA CLA, 4, R TO ACCUMULATOR
5080 DATA CMP, 1, TEST R
5090 DATA TZE, 16, GO TO STOP
5100 DATA MPY, 2,  MULT BY 2
5110 DATA MPY, 3,  MULT BY 3.1416
5120 DATA STA, 5, STORE C
5130 DATA PRT, 4, PRINT R
5140 DATA PRL, 5, PRINT C
5150 DATA TRU, 6, GO BACK
5160 DATA STP, 0, STOP RUN
5170 DATA END, 0, LAST STATEMENT
5180 DATA 1,2,3,4,5,0
```

The operations shown and their meanings are:

DEF Define a constant or a place to store a value
CLA Clear the accumulator and add a value to it
STA Store away the contents of the accumulator
RED Read a value from the DATA statement
CMP Compare the value in the accumulator
TZE Transfer if the CMP test gave a zero result
MPY Multiply the contents of the accumulator
PRT Print a value on a line (not the last)
PRL Print the last value on a line
TRU Transfer unconditionally
STP Stop program
END Last statement of the program

Chapter 20

PLOTTING

The TAB feature permits you to write programs with output in the form of graphs. In order to understand how this is done, you should know that teletype paper has 75 columns available for printing; these positions are ordinarily numbered 1 through 75, but for plotting, they must be considered numbered 0 through 74. It is possible to print 10 characters per inch. The teletype prints 6 lines per inch down the length of the paper. The first problem in this chapter is to plot this table of temperature fluctuations on July 7,1971:

TIME	TEMPERATURE
0000	59.1
0100	57.2
0200	57.8
0300	58.2
0400	57.3
0500	53.8
0600	52.9
0700	52.7
0800	52.3
0900	53.6
1000	58.4
1100	67.9

(Continued on next page)

193

TIME	TEMPERATURE
1200	75.4
1300	84.7
1400	86.4
1500	85.8
1600	84.7
1700	87.9
1800	88.3
1900	89.9
2000	78.1
2100	73.3
2200	68.6
2300	64.3
2400	62.7

We can read the data, then plan our output so that it will cover a span of 50 to 100 degrees. The span is 50 degrees, but there are 75 print positions on the teletype paper; therefore, each degree can be represented by an average of 1.5 print positions.

This flowchart shows how we can plot the data:

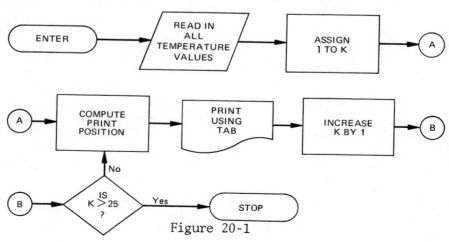

Figure 20-1

The coding is this:

```
10   DIM T(25)
20   FOR K = 1 TO 25
30   READ T(K)
40   NEXT K
50   FOR K = 1 TO 25
60   LET P = INT((((T(K) - 50)/50) * 75)
70   PRINT TAB(P);"*"
80   NEXT K
100 DATA 59.1, 57.2, 57.8, 58.2, 57.3, 53.8, 52.9
110 DATA 52.7, 52.3, 53.6, 58.4, 67.9, 75.4, 84.7
120 DATA 86.4, 85.8, 84.7, 87.9, 88.3, 89.9, 78.1
130 DATA 73.3, 68.6, 64.3, 62.7
```

The printout:

EX20-1   13:36   03 THU 07/15/71

TAB is a built-in function which tabulates the carriage
of the typewriter to the position shown in the function's argument. That argument should, of course, always be a positive
integer. The computer will print the next value beginning at
that point.

In the example, P's value is a simple ratio, expressed as an integer, between the temperature to be printed and the span of temperatures involved times the 75 print positions available.

In the TAB instruction, P keeps changing, thus causing the teletypewriter to print *'s in various places on each line.

The output shows no scalar information. This can easily be provided by inserting a few statements and changing one. Note lines 1, 2, 65, and 70 in the next listing. The statements at lines 1 and 2 set up a horizontal scale and line 70 provides a vertical scale. Line 65 moves the graph eight positions to the right.

```
1    PRINT "        50          60              70";
2    PRINT "               80          90"
10   DIM T(25)
20   FOR K = 1 TO 25
30   READ T(K)
40   NEXT K
50   FOR K = 1 TO 25
60   LET P = INT(((T(K) - 50)/50) * 75)
65   LET P = P + 8
70   PRINT K * 100 - 100; TAB(P); "*"
80   NEXT K
100  DATA 59.1, 57.2, 57.8, 58.2, 57.3, 53.8, 52.9
110  DATA 52.7, 52.3, 53.6, 58.4, 67.9, 75.4, 84.7
120  DATA 86.4, 85.8, 84.7, 87.9, 88.3, 89.9, 78.1
130  DATA 73.3, 68.6, 64.3, 62.7
```

The output is shown on the next page.

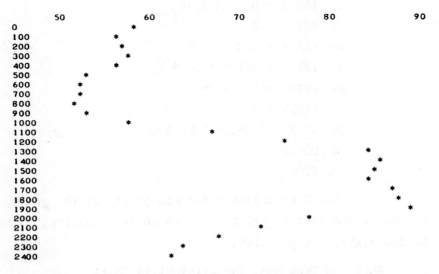

Teletype graphs cannot be very accurate. With only 75 print positions available, the computer can't show small differences between temperatures. They are adequate for applications where only rough indications of trends are needed.

As an exercise, the reader should change the above program so that list T is not needed.

You can see that the TAB command can be placed at various places within a print statement, or not at all. Consider this example:

```
40   PRINT TAB (10); A;B;TAB(50); "*"
```

The computer will type the *value* of A beginning at print position 10; the value of B immediately to the right and, finally, an asterisk in print position 50.

Here are a couple of programs and printouts which require no flowcharts:

```
10   LET M = 36
20   LET I = 6.283185/40
30   LET X = 0
40   LET Y = SIN(X)
50   LET P = INT(M + 36 * Y)
60   PRINT TAB (P);"*"
70   LET X = X + I
80   IF X > 6.28319 THEN 100
90   GO TO 40
100  STOP
```

The value M establishes the mid-point for the graph. Points to the left of print position 36 are negative; those to the right, are positive.

When you type RUN, the printout is this:

EX20-3   14:13   03 THU 04/15/71

This is, of course, the sine curve.

Two curves can be superimposed. Below are shown the sine and cosine curves.

EX20-4   14:21   03 TUE 04/20/71

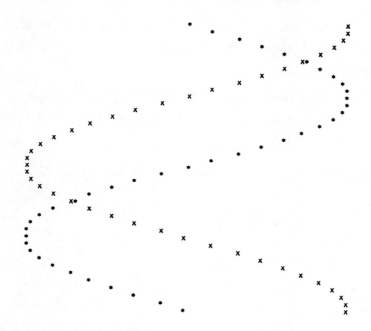

This is the program:

```
10   LET M = 36
20   LET I = 6.283185/40
30   LET X = 0
40   LET S1 = SIN(X)
50   LET S2 = COS(X)
60   LET P1 = INT(M + 36 * S1)
70   LET P2 = INT(M + 36 * S2)
80   IF P2 > P1 THEN 110
90   PRINT TAB(P2); "X"; TAB(P1); "*"
100  GO TO 120
110  PRINT TAB(P1); "*"; TAB(P2); "X"
```

(Continued on next page)

199

```
120 LET X = X + I
130 IF X > 6.28319 THEN 150
140 GO TO 40
150 STOP
```

Note carefully, the decision which is made at line 80. Note also that there are two print statements, one at line 90 and one at line 110.

Here is a program which graphs a circle. Since $X^2 + Y^2 = 1$; Y must equal $1 - X^2$. The curve is plotted from X = -1 to X = +1:

EX20-5   15:11   03 TUE 04/20/71

The program is:

```
10   LET M = 36
20   LET I = 2/40
30   LET X = -1
40   LET Y = SQR(1 - X ↑ 2)
50   LET P1 = INT(M - 34 * Y)
60   LET P2 = INT(M + 34 * Y)
70   PRINT TAB (P1); "*"; TAB(P2); "*"
80   LET X = X + .05
90   IF X > 1 THEN 110
100 GO TO 40
110 STOP
```

****

BASIC MINI-LESSON:

The TAB command, when used in conjunction with the PRINT statement, tabulates the carriage of the teletypewriter to the print position specified. Example:

```
20 PRINT TAB(15);X
30 PRINT TAB(K);D;E;TAB(L);F
```

The command in line 20 causes the carriage of the teletypewriter to be moved to print position 15. Then the value of X is printed.

The command in line 30 causes the carriage of the teletypewriter to be moved to the print position indicated by the value of K. Then the value D is printed. To the right of D, the value of E is printed. Then the carriage moves to the print position indicated by the value of L and the value of F is printed.

It makes a difference whether the value to be printed

is positive or negative. Negative values always begin at the exact point to which the carriage has tabulated; positive values print one position to the right.

   If the argument of the TAB function is not an integer, the computer forms a positive integer from the value. For example, if the argument is 3.6, the system tabulates to position 3; if the argument is -2.4, the system tabulates to position 0 (zero). *Any* negative argument is converted to indicate print position zero.

EXERCISES:

1. Write a program which plots the natural log curve from X = .1 to X = 5. Label the horizontal and vertical scales.

2. Write a program which plots the curve $y = x^2$ from X = -5 to X = +5. Label the horizontal and vertical scales.

3. Write a program which plots the curve $y = 3x^2 - 7x + 1$ from X = -3 to X = 5. Label the horizontal and verticale scales.

Chapter 21

UPHILL/DOWNHILL CLIMBS

Here's another problem. Imagine you're a computer programmer. An engineer visits you in your office and describes
a problem. He says he is working with this equation:

$$H = ae^{-.01[(x-b)^2 + (c-y)^2]}$$

He needs to know which values of x and y will make H
largest when a = 20, b = 11.116 and c = 10.894. The symbol
e is the constant 2.71828. The engineer assures you there is
only *one* largest value for H and that x and y are greater
than 0, but equal to or less than 100.

You ponder about this problem for a while and then hit
upon a scheme you think will work. You picture a field looking like this:

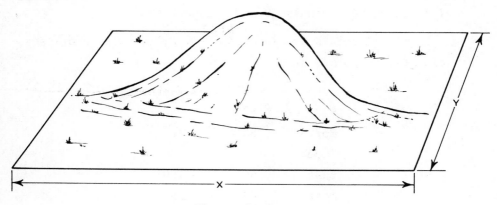

Figure 21-1

On the field there is a hill with just one highest point. The rest of the field slopes uniformly everywhere.

Now suppose we could have the computer select a point (P) on that field and consider the terrain around it. Imagine the field appearing like this:

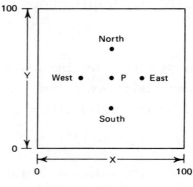

Figure 21-2

As you can see, there are four points around P. They are labeled *North, South, East, West*. Each point is at an equal distance from P.

Each point has an "address." That is, P may be located where X equals 50 and Y equals 50. The point *North* may be located where X equals 50 and y equals 60.

If all points are 10 units from P, then the addresses of the five points are:

	X	Y
P	50	50
North	50	60
South	50	40
East	60	50
West	40	50

We can plug these values of X and Y in the equation

$$H = al^{-.01[(b-x)^2 + (c-y)^2]}$$

and have the program work out the equation 5 times. Since there is only one hilltop on the field, one of the h values will be found to be greatest. We can now have the computer move the entire 5-point grid in the direction indicated by the largest H.

Suppose the first time the program examines the five points, it finds that point *West* (X = 40, Y = 50) gives the largest value. The program will move the 5-point grid to the left. The new addresses of all 5 points are:

P	40	50
North	40	60
South	40	40
East	50	50
West	30	50

Again the program will seek a direction and again will shift the 5-point grid in the correct direction. Eventually the program "brackets" the top of the hill. That is, the 5-point grid will lay over the hill's top, (point P will show the largest h value).

We are not yet ready to print out the values of X and Y because the mesh of the 5-point grid is too large. We know the program has found the *approximate* vicinity for the hilltop but the program has to pin-point its exact location.

The program's procedure must now be to cut the mesh in half and resume the search for the hilltop. The 5-point grid may again roam the field in the vicinity of the hilltop. Again, the program will bracket the hilltop, this time with

205

a finer mesh. The mesh gets cut in half again. The program can be written so that the mesh can be repeatedly cut to so some arbitrary fineness. In our program let's reduce it so that each point is no farther from P than .001.

When the program finds that point P gives the largest value for h, and the mesh need not be reduced further, then the program may assume the hill's top has been found. We can then have the program print the values of X and Y which constitute P's address. Let's flowchart the problem:

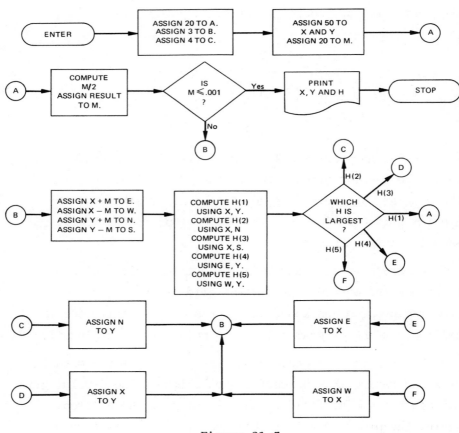

Figure 21-3

In this program, an initial assignment of 20 is made to M, the mesh size. You can see, though, that it is immediately cut in half. The flowchart shows that whenever H(1) is largest, the mesh will again be cut in half.

The symbols N, S, E, W stand for North, South, East and West, respectively. Observe how the points around the central point P are established by modifying the values assigned to the central point. That is, the values assigned to X and Y establish the central point while X + M, X - M, Y + M, Y - M establish the surrounding points.

Observe that during any one iteration point the largest value of H tells in which direction to walk. Only one value X, or Y must be changed to indicate a new central point. For instance, when H(2) is largest, the new central point is located to the north of the old central point. The value of X does not change but the value of Y does. The new value of Y is N.

Here is the program:

```
10   DIM H(5)
20   LET A = 20
30   LET B = 11.116
40   LET C = 10.894
50   LET X = 50
55   LET Y = 50
60   LET M = 20
70   LET M = M/2
80   IF M <= .001 THEN 700
90   LET E = X + M
100  LET W = X - M
110  LET N = Y + M
```

(Continued on next page)

```
120 LET S = Y - M
130 LET H(1) = A * EXP(-.01*((B-X)↑2+(C-Y)↑2))
140 LET H(2) = A * EXP(-.01*((B-X)↑2+(C-N)↑2))
150 LET H(3) = A * EXP(-.01*((B-X)↑2+(C-S)↑2))
160 LET H(4) = A * EXP(-.01*((B-E)↑2+(C-Y)↑2))
170 LET H(5) = A * EXP(-.01*((B-W)↑2+(C-Y)↑2))
180 LET G = H(1)
190 LET J = 1
200 FOR I = 2 TO 5
210 IF H(I) > G THEN 214
212 GO TO 220
214 LET G = H(I)
216 LET J = I
220 NEXT I
230 ON J GO TO 70, 300, 400, 500, 600
300 LET Y = N
310 GO TO 90
400 LET Y = S
410 GO TO 90
500 LET X = E
510 GO TO 90
600 LET X = W
610 GO TO 90
700 PRINT "FOUND TOP OF HILL. IT IS WHERE X=";
705 PRINT X;" AND Y= ";Y
710 PRINT "VALUE OF H AT THAT POINT IS ";G
RUN
```

The printout is this:

EX21-1   16:32   03 TUE 04/20/71

FOUND TOP OF HILL. IT IS WHERE X = 11.1157 AND Y = 10.8936
VALUE OF H AT THAT POINT IS   20

If you want to plot the path that the program takes as it moves from X = 50, Y = 50 to X = 11.1157, Y = 10.8936, add these statements:

```
300 PRINT "MOVED NORTH TO", X, N
305 LET Y = N
400 PRINT "MOVED SOUTH TO", X, S
405 LET Y = S
500 PRINT "MOVED EAST TO", E, Y
505 LET X = E
600 PRINT "MOVED WEST TO", W, Y
605 LET X = W
```

When you type RUN, you get this output:

EX21-2   16:34   03 TUE 04/20/71

MOVED SOUTH TO	50	40
MOVED WEST TO	40	40
MOVED SOUTH TO	40	30
MOVED WEST TO	30	30
MOVED SOUTH TO	30	20
MOVED WEST TO	20	20
MOVED SOUTH TO	20	10
MOVED WEST TO	10	10
MOVED EAST TO	11.25	10
MOVED NORTH TO	11.25	11.25
MOVED SOUTH TO	11.25	10.625
MOVED NORTH TO	11.25	10.9375
MOVED WEST TO	11.0938	10.9375
MOVED SOUTH TO	11.0938	10.8594
MOVED NORTH TO	11.0938	10.8984
MOVED EAST TO	11.1328	10.8984
MOVED WEST TO	11.1133	10.8984

(Continued on next page)

209

```
MOVED SOUTH TO    11.1133           10.8936
MOVED EAST TO     11.1182           10.8936
MOVED WEST TO     11.1157           10.8936
FOUND TOP OF HILL. IT IS WHERE X = 11.1157 AND Y = 10.8936
VALUE OF H AT THAT POINT IS 20
```

Each line of the printout shows the direction in which the grid moved. Also, it tells the X and Y co-ordinates of the grid's mid-point.

By studying the original equation, mathematicians can tell you that the actual values of X and Y are 11.116 and 10.894, not 11.1157 and 10.8936 shown. As we've said before, the computer is a finite device and sometimes can't express answers to the very last decimal place. Most of the time, this shouldn't concern you. An engineer will accept the above solution to this problem. He would probably round off the answers anyway.

You can now see that the equation itself had the answers to the problem:

$$H = ae^{-.01[(b-x)^2 + (c-y)^2]}$$

The value a gives the height of the hill; b and c give the X and Y co-ordinates at the point where the hilltop is located.

The problem could, therefore, have been solved by mathemactical analysis rather than by a computer program. This points up the fact that sometimes, if the programmer is clever, a program is not necessary to solve a problem.

Nevertheless, you will encounter many problems where a "hill-climbing" technique similar to the one shown in the last example is needed.

Naturally, there's much more to hill-climbing techniques that what we've shown here. There are problems and pitfalls which we haven't space to discuss. Be sure to analyze your problem carefully and thoroughly when you feel a hill-climbing technique is needed. Consult a mathematician when you must.

EXERCISES:

1. Change the parameters in the equation given on page 203 to see how the program works under various conditions.

2. Change the equation itself to see what effect doing this has on the program.

Chapter 22

FILE MAINTENANCE

Let's take a typical business situation. Assume that in Company X there is a reel of magnetic tape containing information about every employee of the company. The information gives each employee's name, home address, social security number, pay number, work station, job description, pay rate, number of dependents, and many other items of a similar nature.

The information on the tape constitutes a "master file." Master files are often stored on magnetic tape because one reel of tape can contain great quantities of information. This information can be processed by a computer to help generate reports, pay checks, or studies.

The information in master files is stored in the form of records. Where personnel files are concerned, each record gives all the information about one person; where inventory files are concerned, each record gives all the information about one part.

Let's suppose the records are all the same size. This isn't always true, but such an assumption is OK for this example. Here is the important point: the information concerning one person is in the same relative position in any one record that the information concerning another person is in another record.

Here's an example:

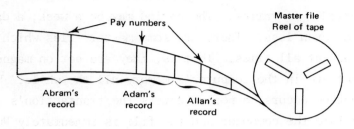

Figure 22-1

The illustrated reel contains hundreds, if not thousands, of records. Note that in this illustration the pay number for each person appears at approximately mid-point in each record. Other items of information (not shown) in other records appear in identical relative positions.

A master file is up-to-date only for a very short period of time, perhaps only an hour after it has been generated. Within that hour, a person may write a note to his supervisor like this:

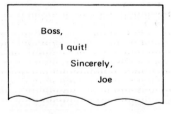

Figure 22-2

A "transaction" has occurred which affects the master file. The file is no longer up-to-date. When a transaction occurs, one doesn't walk over to the computer and create a new master file. This would be grossly uneconomical.

213

Instead, transactions are "batched," i.e., they're saved.

The period of time during which transactions are batched is called a "batching period." How long is a batching period? It varies. The period may be a week, a day, an hour, or even less. There are some master files which are "on-line" at all times. That is, they are not on magnetic tape but are in the computer's memory all the while. When a transaction occurs, a person enters the transaction's information into the computer and the file is immediately "updated." Continuous updating of master files is becoming more and more important in the business world as time goes on.

Usually, transactions are initially recorded on pieces of paper called "source documents." Joe's note was an example of a source document. Other kinds of source documents take such forms as pension-plan authorizations, personnel forms for people newly hired, change-of-address forms, and others. These source documents are saved until one-week's worth have been collected. Then data processing cards are punched by keypunch operators; each card containing the information found on one source document. Here's an example:

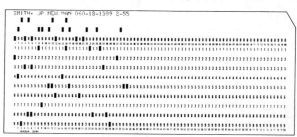

Figure 22-3

A deck of data processing cards is generated which contains the week's transactions. These cards are taken to a mechanical sorter which sorts the cards according to some

214

item of information on each card. That field is called a
"key." The key upon which the cards are sorted may be employee name (alphabetically), pay number or Social Security
number (numerically), or perhaps some other data item.

The key used to sort transactions must be the *same key*
that the master file is sorted on. It makes little difference what the key is so long as records on the master file
and transaction records are sorted the same way.

After transactions have been sorted, the cards are
taken to another machine called a "card-to-tape converter."
The cards, comprising the batched transactions, are recorded
on magnetic tape. That reel of tape is called the "transaction file."

Sorting is performed so that the master file can be updated efficiently. We'll see why this is true presently. We
should point out that the transaction file can be recorded
on magnetic tape without first being sorted on a mechanical
sorter. The computer, itself, can be used for sorting during
the actual file updating. Whether a batch of transactions is
sorted mechanically or by computer, depends upon the econom-
ics of the situation. Whichever method is cheaper is the
method which is used. Generally, the larger the number of
transactions, the more the likelihood that a computer should
be used.

Having created a transaction file, we are now ready to
update our master file. This updating is done by a computer.
Figure 22-4 is an illustration showing how it's done.

You can see that three reels of tape are involved, the
master file to be updated, the transaction file, and a blank
reel of tape. The idea is this: a small part of the master

215

file is brought into the computer's memory. A small part of the transaction file is also brought into the computer's memory. The computer then tries to make "matches" between records in the master file and records in the transaction file.

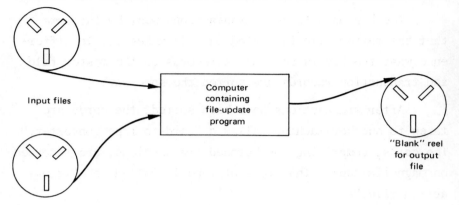

Input files

Computer containing file-update program

"Blank" reel for output file

Figure 22-4

If a master file record is brought into memory and no matching transaction file record is found, the computer knows that no change is to be made in that file record. That master file record is *copied* on the blank reel exactly as it was on the master reel.

If a matching transaction record is found in the transaction file, the appropriate changes are made to the master record *in the computer's memory*; then the changed record is written out on the blank reel.

If the transaction file record shows that a master file record is to be deleted from the master file, that record is simply *not* written out on the blank reel. Suppose Joe quits, for example, the new master file being generated will not contain a record concerning him.

Because both master and transaction files are sorted on the same key, the computer never has to look very far to determine whether a master file record has a matching transaction file record. No match means "copy the master file record exactly as is;" a match means "change the record before copying it," or "drop it entirely." The transaction record, itself, tells which function to perform: to change and copy or to drop.

When all of the records in the master file and all of the records in the transaction file have been read, the records appearing on what was originally a blank reel, constitute the new master file. This new master file contains up-to-date information concerning all the personnel in the organization. That new master file will, in turn, be updated at the end of another batching period.

Traditionally, in file maintenance operations, reels of tape have acquired certain picturesque names. The old master file in a file-update situation is known as the "father" tape, the new master file is known as the "son" tape.

During the next update run, the "son" tape is renamed "father," the "father" is renamed "grandfather." The new master file is named "son." In case of trouble with the current father tape, it will be possible to dig out the "grandfather" tape (and its associated transaction file) and regenerate the faulty father tape.

The BASIC programming language has no command which deal with magnetic tapes but it does have commands which enable users to work with files. The commands are FILES, READ, WRITE, BACKSPACE, SCRATCH, RESTORE, IF END.

What is a file? In time-sharing mode, a file is a saved "program" containing data. That data may be numeric or alphanumeric. A file, like a program, consists of numbered lines. The word DATA is optional on each line. We won't use the word in examples.

Let's set up a file. Here is the conversation between you and the computer. The underlined words are those typed by the computer:

SYSTEM--BASIC
NEW OR OLD--NEW
NEW FILE NAME--INFILE
READY.

10	16.2	18.7	9.4
20	3	42.8	99
30	17	4	

SAVE
READY.

We've created a file called INFILE. It has three lines numbered 10, 20 and 30. The lines contain a total of eight values.

Note that the values are not separated by commas. Commas are optional. In these examples, we'll use spaces to separate numeric values. One or more spaces between numbers are OK.

This file is called INFILE. A file *name* may be made up of from one to six characters. Those characters don't all have to be alphabetic, but the rules about which characters you may use are tricky, and we'd advise you to always make up alphabetic file names.

Note the command SAVE. This command causes your file to be saved. That file can now be accessed by other programs.

Let's write a main program which uses INFILE. (In order to distinguish programs from files, we'll refer to programs which call for and use files as *main programs*.)

Study this example:

```
10 FILES INFILE
20 READ #1,X
30 PRINT X;
40 IF END #1 THEN 60
50 GO TO 20
60 PRINT
70 PRINT "NO MORE VALUES IN INFILE"
RUN
```

The output looks like this:

```
EX22-1          16:08      03 TUE 04/20/71

 16.2   18.7   9.4   3   42.8   99   17   4
NO MORE VALUES IN INFILE
```

A user must *declare* what files are to be used in his program. Study line 10. The user is telling the computer that INFILE is a file to be used. In the next line, the reference to #1 is a reference to INFILE.

Suppose a main program reads:

```
10 FILES ALPHA; BETA; GAMMA
```

There are three files to be used. They are ALPHA, BETA and GAMMA. Those files must have been saved before the main program may use them. The main program refers to the files as #1, #2, and #3. ALPHA is #1, BETA is #2 and GAMMA is #3.

Note that the FILES command in line 10 separates the file names with semicolons, not commas. This is very

219

important; commas won't work.

Place the FILES command at the very beginning of your program. It *must* go there.

The command, IF END, tests a file to see whether it contains more unused data values. If the file contains no more data values, the IF END command causes the computer to take the jump shown in the command. A good place to put the IF END command is immediately ahead of the file, READ statement. When the program executes IF END #1, it looks in INFILE to see whether all values have been used. If so, the program jumps to line 60. If not, the program advances to the next line of the main program and reads INFILE.

You saw from the above printout that the read-file command picks up values from the named file. Those instructions ignore line numbers in the data file. However, the data values are considered to be in one continuous data line; that is, when one data line is exhausted, the program goes to the next.

One can *write* into a file as well as read from one. Space to write into a file must be saved ahead of time. Let's save space in the form of a file. We'll name the file OUTFIL. We do this by typing:

```
OLD
OLD FILE NAME--CH1536***
READY.
RENAME
NEW FILE NAME--OUTFIL
READY.
SAVE
READY.
```

The computer's part of the conversation is shown under-lined. What happens is this: we ask for *file space* using the *standard* file name CH1536***. Then, since we're not per-mitted to use a file with that name, we rename it OUTFIL. The file space is now available to the main program which uses OUTFIL.

OUTFIL is a "blank" file. This means that space has been reserved but nothing has been written into that space yet.

Parenthetically, we'll point out that there are six standard files a user may select from. They are CH0192***, CH0384***, CH0768***, CH1536***, CH3072***, CH6144***. The numbers within the file names give the relative sizes of the files. The first is very small; the last is the largest. You should select a file size to suit the requirements of your problem.

Now let's use files INFILE and OUTFIL in a program:

```
10 FILES INFILE;OUTFIL
20 SCRATCH #2
30 IF END #1 THEN 70
40 READ #1,X
50 WRITE #2,X
60 GO TO 30
70 PRINT "NO MORE VALUES IN INFILE"
RUN
```

Here is the output from the program run:

EX22-2   16:15   03 TUE 04/20/71

NO MORE VALUES IN INFILE

This program reads sequential values of X from INFILE and writes them in OUTFIL.

What do you suppose SCRATCH does (line 20)? This statement prepares a file for writing. It's a protective device forcing a user to think twice about writing into a file. It would be a disaster, for example, for a program to write into input file #1, for example, when the intent was to write into output file #2. The system will not allow the writing into a file unless it has been scratched.

If a WRITE command names more than one data item, those data items must be separated by semicolons. Remember this, you'll get error messages otherwise. For example, type your WRITE statements like this:

30 WRITE #2, P; Q; R; X; Y; Z

Note that there's a comma following the file number but semicolons separating data items.

How do we know whether our last program run was successful? We must list OUTFIL. After the main program has stopped we can call for a listing of OUTFIL this way:

OLD
OLD FILE NAME--OUTFIL
READY.
LIST

The computer will type this:

OUTFIL	16:19	03 TUE 04/20/71
1000	16.2	
1010	18.7	
1020	9.4	
1030	3	
1040	42.8	
1050	99	
1060	17	
1070	4	

There's another way to get a printout which you may like better. When your main program has stopped, you may type:

EDIT PAGE INFILE, OUTFIL

This command will neatly print out the current contents of all programs or files named (up to nine) in the list. The output from the above command looks like this:

INFILE

10	16.2	18.7	9.4
20	3	42.8	99
30	17	4	

OUTFIL

1000	16.2
1010	18.7
1020	9.4
1030	3
1040	42.8
1050	99
1060	17
1070	4

For every WRITE command which was executed, the program generated one line in the output file. The system automatically assigned line numbers, beginning with 1000, to the data in the output file.

EDIT PAGE is a useful command since the output is in the form of numbered 8 1/2" x 11" pages. These pages may be torn from the teletypewriter, punched and inserted in a notebook.

Here are a few facts about files which you need to know. There are two modes that files may be in: *read* and *write*. Initially, all files are in the read mode. You can change a file from read to write by using the SCRATCH command. You saw how this is done in an earlier example.

A file can be changed from write mode to read mode by having the computer execute the RESTORE command. This means that if you have written a file in one portion of a program and you wish to read it in another portion, the program must execute RESTORE before it can read that file. Example:

50 RESTORE #2

RESTORE has another use. It permits a program to begin reading a file again from the beginning.

BACKSPACE is a command which backs up the referenced file one data item at a time. Only files in the read mode can be backspaced. BACKSPACE can be used when data must be processed from end to beginning. Example:

80 BACKSPACE #1

****

BASIC MINI-LESSON:

This is a summary of the file handling commands in BASIC:

FILES. You name the files used in your main program. Separate names with semicolons. In the main program, files are numbered according to the sequence the files are listed in the FILES command.

READ. Files may be read. Example:

60 READ #1,A,B,C

WRITE. Files may be written into. Example:

170 WRITE #3,X;Y;Z

SCRATCH. This command changes a file from its normal *read*
mode to *write* mode. A file must be in write mode before it can be written into.

BACKSPACE. The data in a file in read mode may be backspaced
one item at a time.

RESTORE. The data in a file in read mode may be reread from
the beginning. RESTORE also changes a file from
write to read mode.

IF END. A file may be tested to determine whether there are
more unused data items stored. Example:

80 IF END #2 THEN 200

The program will go to line 200 if there are no more
data items in file #2. Otherwise, it will go to the
next statement in sequence.

Space may be assigned for output files by using standard files CH0192***, CH0384***, CH0768***, CH1536***,
CH3072***, CH6144***.

EDIT PAGE permits listing up to 9 programs or files in
8 1/2" x 11" format. The command may be given at any time
the user has a program in memory. That program need not be
one which he lists. After the listing has taken place, the
program which the user placed in memory is still there, unchanged.

Chapter 23

A FILE UPDATE CASE STUDY

Suppose you want to set up a file which is to contain up-to-date information about your parts inventory. For simplicity, let's say that each record of the file will contain only a part number and a quantity-on-hand. Let's call the file MASTER. Here's how you set it up:

```
NEW
NEW FILE NAME--MASTER
READY.
10    1240    35
20    1246    90
30    1248    105
40    1260    281
50    1263    17
60    1267    26
70    1271    86
80    1276    900
90    1280    0
100   1286    46
110   1288    180
120   1294    16
130   1296    20
140   1297    82
150   1299    65
SAVE
READY.
```

The underlined entries are typed by the system - you type the others.

The first column contains line numbers; the second, part numbers; the third, quantities-on-hand. There are only 15 part records in the file but, of course, in real life, there could be thousands.

Suppose you need to update the master file with these transactions:

PART NUMBER	TRANSACTION
1246	Subtract 30 parts
1260	Add 100 parts
1271	Add 10 parts
1280	Add 50 parts
1294	Subtract 2 parts
1286	Delete the entire record from the master file
1297	Delete the entire record from the master file
1250	Incorporate a new record in the master file (130 parts)
1275	Incorporate a new record in the master file (26 parts)
1306	Incorporate a new record in the master file (17 parts)
1296	Add 15 parts
1240	Add 43 parts

You may enter these transactions in a transaction file. Let's call the file TRANS. Here's the way it's done:

NEW
NEW FILE NAME--TRANS
READY.

(Continued on next page)

227

```
10    1246    CHANGE    -30
20    1260    CHANGE    100
30    1271    CHANGE    10
40    1280    CHANGE    50
50    1294    CHANGE    -2
60    1286    DELETE    0
70    1297    DELETE    0
80    1247    CHANGE    10
90    1250    NEW       130
100   1275    NEX       25
110   1305    ADD       26
120   1306    NEW       17
130   1296    NEW       15
140   1240    CHANGW    43
SAVE
READY.
```

Each record has four entries. The first column contains line numbers; the second, part numbers; the third, transaction codes; the fourth, quantities. Observe that there are several clerical errors in the transaction file. Only three kinds of transactions are possible: CHANGE, DELETE, NEW. You'll see that CHANGE and NEW have been misspelled and that an illegal word (ADD) has been used. In line 130, the word NEW is incorrectly used instead of CHANGE, which is correct.

The meanings of the transaction codes are:

CHANGE   The quantity shown in the record is
                added to the corresponding master file
                record (if positive) or subtracted
                from the corresponding master file rec-
                ord (if negative).

228

DELETE   The entire record is to be dropped from
              the master file. A value in the quantity
              column must be included and it must be
              zero.

NEW   The record (except for transaction code)
              must be incorporated into the master file.
              The value in the quantity column gives the
              quantity-on-hand for the new record.

The problem which we'll solve in this chapter is two-fold:

1.   We'll sort the transaction file (TRANS) and store the
     sorted records in a new file TRANSS for sorting. We'll
     use the Shell Method.

2.   We'll update the master file in the traditional sense;
     that is, by reading records from MASTER and TRANSS, per-
     forming the transactions indicated by the transaction
     code found in TRANSS, and creating a new updated file
     NMF. (NMF stands for *new master file*.)

The program which sorts TRANS will be called SORT; the
program which updates the master file will be called UPDATE.
The latter program must not only create NMF but it must also
check for errors. In real life, a file update program must
check for scores of different kinds of errors, such as dup-
lications, missing information, records out of sequence, etc.
For simplicity, our program will check for only three kinds
of errors. They are:

1.   Illegal or incorrectly spelled transaction code.

2.   Illogical transaction code. A transaction record has
     no matching master file record but the transaction code
     is not labeled NEW, as it should be.

229

3. Part numbers match in the master and transaction file records, but the transaction code is incorrectly labeled NEW. The code may only be CHANGE or DELETE.

As a challenging exercise, write the SORT program. You may assume that all of the transaction file (TRANS) can be brought into memory and that there are no more than 100 records in the file. Have the program store the sorted records in file TRANSS. When the sort is completed, have the program type the message END OF SORT.

Here are some hints which should prove helpful.

1. Modify, as required, the Shell Method given in an earlier chapter.

2. Use this statement in your program:

   DIM P(100), C$(100), Q(100)

   P means part number
   C$ means transaction code
   Q means quantity-on-hand

3. Use this READ statement to bring TRANS records into memory:

   READ #1, P(I), C$(I), Q(I)

4. Use this WRITE statement to write sorted records into TRANSS:

   WRITE #2, P(I); C$(I); Q(I)

Keep in mind that you must have the program execute SCRATCH #2 before the program will write into file #2 (TRANSS).

5. Be sure your program declares files TRANS and TRANSS at the very beginning of your sort program.

6. Set up space for file #2 (TRANSS) by using these commands:

      OLD

      OLD FILE NAME--CH1536***

      READY.

      RENAME

      NEW FILE NAME--TRANSS

      READY.

      SAVE

      READY.

Your sort program is to read into memory all records from file #1 (TRANS). If there are more than 100 records in the file, the program must print a message saying so, then it must stop. Be sure your program counts the number of records actually read from TRANS so that the number can be assigned to N, a value which the Shell Method requires in order to work properly.

Do not read beyond this point until you have made an attempt to write the sort program. Below is one possible solution:

```
10   FILES TRANS;TRANSS
15   LET N = 0
20   DIM P(100), C$(100), Q(100)
30   FOR I = 1 TO 100
40   IF END #1 THEN 180
50   READ #1,P(I),C$(I),Q(I)
60   LET N = N + 1
61   NEXT I
62   PRINT "TOO MANY RECORDS IN FILE TO SORT"
```

(Continued on next page)

231

```
63   STOP
180  LET D = 1
190  LET D = D * 2
200  LET J = INT(N/D)
210  IF J = 0 THEN 440
220  LET L = 1
230  LET H = 1 + J
240  IF H > N THEN 190
250  LET L1 = L
260  LET H1 = H
270  IF P(H) >= P(L) THEN 390
280  LET T = P(L)
281  LET U$ = C$(L)
282  LET T2 = Q(L)
290  LET P(L) = P(H)
291  LET C$(L) = C$(H)
292  LET Q(L) = Q(H)
300  LET P(H) = T
301  LET C$(H) = U$
302  LET Q(H) = T2
350  LET L = L-J
360  IF L < 1 THEN 390
370  LET H = H - J
380  GO TO 270
390  LET L = L1
400  LET H = H1
410  LET L = L + 1
420  LET H = H + 1
430  GO TO 240
440  SCRATCH #2
441  FOR I = 1 TO N
```

(Continued on next page)

```
450 WRITE #2,P(I);C$(I);Q(I)
460 NEXT I
470 PRINT "END OF SORT"
```

When you type RUN, you get this output:

SORT   8:03   03 THU 04/22/71

END OF SORT

The transaction file has now been sorted. Let's compare
TRANS with TRANSS to see whether the sort has indeed been
successful. Here are listings of TRANS and TRANSS. (You obtain listings of files or programs when you type LIST.)

TRANS   12:17   03 THU 04/22/71

10	1246	CHANGE	-30
20	1260	CHANGE	100
30	1271	CHANGE	10
40	1280	CHANGE	50
50	1294	CHANGE	-2
60	1286	DELETE	0
70	1297	DELETE	0
80	1247	CHANGE	10
90	1250	NEW	130
100	1275	NEX	25
110	1305	ADD	26
120	1306	NEW	17
130	1296	NEW	15
140	1240	CHANGW	43

TRANSS   12:18   03 THU 04/22/71

| 1000 | 1240 | CHANGW | 43 |
| 1010 | 1246 | CHANGE | -30 |

(Continued on next page)

233

1020	1247	CHANGE	10
1030	1250	NEW	130
1040	1260	CHANGE	100
1050	1271	CHANGE	10
1060	1275	NEX	25
1070	1280	CHANGE	50
1080	1286	DELETE	0
1090	1294	CHANGE	-2
1100	1296	NEW	15
1110	1297	DELETE	0
1120	1305	ADD	26
1130	1306	NEW	17

You now have two files, MASTER and TRANSS, and are al-most ready to write your file update program. You must pre-pare space for a new master file. Follow this procedure:

```
OLD
OLD FILE NAME--CH3072***
READY.
RENAME
NEW FILE NAME--NMF
READY.
SAVE
READY.
```

The next assignment in this chapter is to develop the flowchart which can be used in your file update program. Do not read beyond this point until you have made an attempt to prepare one.

On the next two pages is a flowchart which may be used.

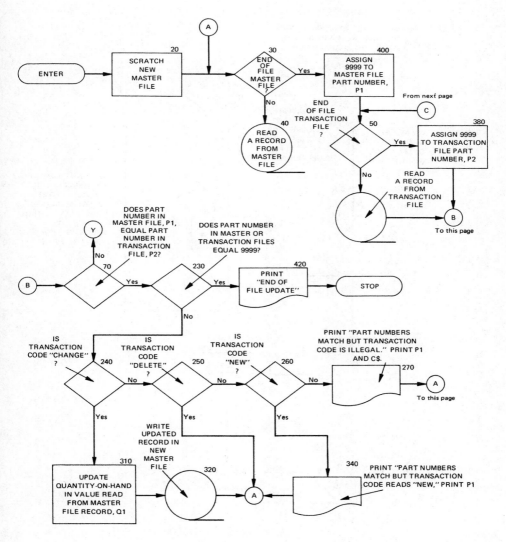

Figure 23-1

235

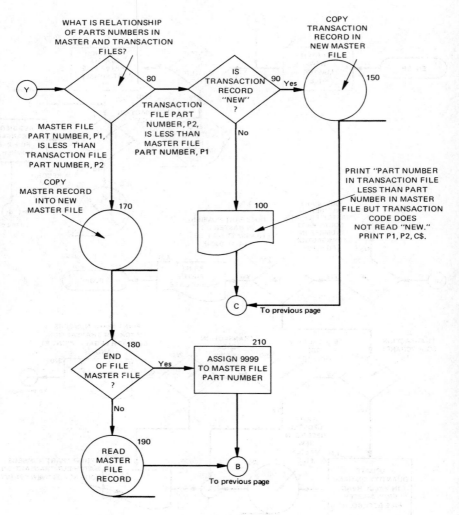

Figure 23-1 (Cont'd)

236

Study the flowchart carefully. You'll see that a number of problems need to be solved. Make sure you know the answers to these questions:

1. What does the program do if master file records run out before transaction file records?

2. What does the program do if transaction file records run out before master file records?

3. What does the program do if a transaction file record has no matching master file record? How does the program find out that a transaction file record has no matching master file record?

4. What does the program do if a master file record has no transaction affecting it? How does the computer find out that a master file record has no transaction?

5. What does the program do if part numbers in master and transaction file records match but the transaction code is "NEW"?

6. How does the program delete a record?

7. How does the program know when the job is done?

Here is one way that UPDATE can be written in accordance with the flowchart:

```
10   FILES MASTER;TRANSS;NMF
20   SCRATCH #3
30   IF END #1 THEN 400
40   READ #1,P1,Q1
50   IF END #2 THEN 380
60   READ #2,P2,C$,Q2
70   IF P1 = P2 THEN 230
```

(Continued on next page)

237

```
80  IF P1 < P2 THEN 170
90  IF C$ = "NEW" THEN 150
100 PRINT "ERROR. PART NUMBER IN TRANSACTION FILE LESS"
110 PRINT "         THAN PART NUMBER IN MASTER FILE BUT"
120 PRINT "         TRANSACTION CODE DOES NOT READ 'NEW'."
130 PRINT "               P1=";P1;" P2=";P2;" CODE=";C$
140 GO TO 50
150 WRITE #3,P2;Q2
160 GO TO 50
170 WRITE #3,P1;Q1
180 IF END #1 THEN 210
190 READ #1,P1,Q1
200 GO TO 70
210 LET P1 = 9999
220 GO TO 70
230 IF P1 = 9999 THEN 420
240 IF C$ = "CHANGE" THEN 310
250 IF C$ = "DELETE" THEN 30
260 IF C$ = "NEW" THEN 340
270 PRINT "ERROR. PART NUMBERS MATCH BUT TRANSACTION CODE"
280 PRINT "         IS ILLEGAL."
290 PRINT "               P1=";P1;" CODE=";C$
300 GO TO 30
310 LET Q1 = Q1 + Q2
320 WRITE #3,P1;Q1
330 GO TO 30
340 PRINT "ERROR. PART NUMBERS MATCH BUT TRANSACTION CODE"
350 PRINT "         READS 'NEW'."
360 PRINT "               P1=";P1'
370 GO TO 30
380 LET P2 = 9999
```

(Continued on next page)

```
390 GO TO 70
400 LET P1 = 9999
410 GO TO 50
420 PRINT "END OF FILE UPDATE"
```

This is the nomenclature:

MASTER	Master file
TRANSS	Sorted transaction file
NMF	New master file
P1	Part number in master file
P2	Part number in transaction file
Q1	Quantity-on-hand in master file
Q2	Quantity in transaction file
C$	Transaction code

We may update our master file in two phases. First by using SORT to sort TRANS, creating TRANSS. Then, by running UPDATE using MASTER and TRANSS to obtain NMF.

When you call for the running of UPDATE, you get this output:

```
UPDATE              13:08      03 THU 04/22/71

ERROR. PART NUMBERS MATCH BUT TRANSACTION CODE
       IS ILLEGAL.
              P1= 1240    CODE=CHANGW
ERROR. PART NUMBER IN TRANSACTION FILE LESS
       THAN PART NUMBER IN MASTER FILE BUT
       TRANSACTION CODE DOES NOT READ 'NEW'.
              P1= 1248  P2= 1247  CODE=CHANGE
ERROR. PART NUMBER IN TRANSACTION FILE LESS
       THAN PART NUMBER IN MASTER FILE BUT
       TRANSACTION CODE DOES NOT READ 'NEW'.
              P1= 1276  P2= 1275  CODE=NEX
```
(Continued on next page)

239

ERROR. PART NUMBERS MATCH BUT TRANSACTION CODE
        READS 'NEW'.
               P1= 1296
ERROR. PART NUMBER IN TRANSACTION FILE LESS
        THAN PART NUMBER IN MASTER FILE BUT
        TRANSACTION CODE DOES NOT READ 'NEW'.
               P1= 9999 P2= 1305 CODE=ADD
END OF FILE UPDATE

It is possible to *chain* SORT and UPDATE. Simply add
this statement to SORT:

        480 CHAIN UPDATE

Now run SORT. The sorting of TRANS will take place, the
program creating TRANSS. Then, the computer will automatically bring UPDATE into memory and run it. This will be the
output:

SORT   13:10   03 THU 04/22/71

END OF SORT
ERROR. PART NUMBERS MATCH BUT TRANSACTION CODE
        IS ILLEGAL.
               P1= 1240 CODE=CHANGE
ERROR. PART NUMBER IN TRANSACTION FILE LESS
        THAN PART NUMBER IN MASTER FILE BUT
        TRANSACTION CODE DOES NOT READ 'NEW'.
               P1= 1248 P2= 1247 CODE=CHANGE
ERROR. PART NUMBER IN TRANSACTION FILE LESS
        THAN PART NUMBER IN MASTER FILE BUT
        TRANSACTION CODE DOES NOT READ 'NEW'.
               P1= 1276 P2= 1275 CODE=NEX
ERROR. PART NUMBERS MATCH BUT TRANSACTION CODE
        READS 'NEW'.
               (Continued on next page)
240

P1= 1296

ERROR. PART NUMBER IN TRANSACTION FILE LESS
THAN PART NUMBER IN MASTER FILE BUT
TRANSACTION CODE DOES NOT READ 'NEW'.

P1= 9999 P2= 1305 CODE=ADD

END OF FILE UPDATE

Now we can list the original file, MASTER, and the updated master, NMF, to determine whether the program works
properly. Here are listings of MASTER and NMF.

MASTER   13:19   03 THU 04/22/71

10	1240	35
20	1246	90
30	1248	105
40	1260	281
50	1263	17
60	1267	26
70	1271	86
80	1276	900
90	1280	0
100	1286	46
110	1288	180
120	1294	16
130	1296	20
140	1297	82
150	1299	65

NMF   13:20   03 THU 04/22/71

1000	1246	60
1010	1248	105
1020	1250	130

(Continued on next page)

241

1030	1260	381
1040	1263	17
1050	1267	26
1060	1271	96
1070	1276	900
1080	1280	50
1090	1288	180
1100	1294	14
1110	1299	65
1120	1306	17

By studying the output you can see that the program gives the expected output except for those records where errors were made in the transaction file.

Part 1240 originally on the master file was dropped from the new master file because the transaction code in the corresponding transaction record was illegal.

Part 1275 was a part to be incorporated in the new master file. The task was not accomplished because the correct transaction code in the corresponding transaction record was incorrectly spelled.

Part 1296 was not updated because the wrong transaction code was given in the corresponding transaction record.

Part 1305 was a part to be incorporated in the new master file. The task was not accomplished because the wrong transaction code was given in the corresponding transaction record.

Corrections may now be made, of course, and the job rerun. Or corrections may be incorporated the next time UPDATE is run. Management decides whether part records should be dropped from the master file when corresponding transaction records are faulty. Would you suggest that instead of cropping part records 1240 and 1296 from the master file, they should be left unchanged until the applicable error messages have been analyzed.

The next time UPDATE is run, the roles played by files MASTER and NMF can be reversed by changing line 10 to read:

    10 FILES NMF;TRANSS;MASTER

Now NMF becomes file #1, the input file, and MASTER becomes file #3, the updated "new" master file.

EXERCISES:

1. Discuss the differences likely to be found between the update program in this chapter and one for a real-life application. How many data items would you expect to find in a record? Would a more than one kind of transaction occur to affect a master record? If so, in what order should the transactions be recorded on the master file?

2. Discuss what is meant by random access. How does updating a file organized for random access differ from updating a file organized for serial access (as described in this chapter)? Why are random access files more suitable in certain situations than serial access files?

3. Records to be sorted usually contain several data items. Consider the file which follows (let's call it FILE-X):

10	170	15	PQR	3	1040
20	151	15	GHI	3	1030
30	145	17	ABC	4	1060
40	168	16	MNO	4	1050
50	165	48	JKL	3	1028
60	150	80	DEF	4	1035
70	180	18	YZZ	6	1090
80	178	25	VWX	1	1035
90	176	31	STU	6	1065

The file contains nine records; each record contains
five data items. (The left-most number in each record is a
line number, not a data item of the record.) Call the data
items in each record A,B,C$,D,E.

Write a program which sorts FILE-X, in ascending sequence, giving sorted records in FILE-Y. The first data item
in each record, A, is the sort key. That is, in the sorted
file, the values of A must be in increasing sequence. Use
the Shell Method.

You'll need this DIM statement in your program:

DIM A(100), B(100), C$(100), D(100), E(100), S(100)

Have the program read into memory all the values of A,
B, C$, D and E. Then have it sort *only the values in list A.*
Have the program record, in list S, the *original positions*
of the A values. After the program has sorted the values in
list A, list S should look like this:

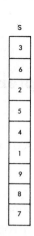

Figure 23-2

Note that in FILE-X, the record at position 3 is the one which must appear as the first record of FILE-Y; that the record at position 6 is the one which must appear as the second record; etc.

The portion of your program which actually creates FILE-Y is written like this:

```
SCRATCH #2
FOR I = 1 TO N
WRITE #2, A(I);B(S(I));C$(S(I));D(S(I));E(S(I))
NEXT I
```

Note that S is the subscript to be used for each of the lists except list A.

When I is 1, the first value in list S is used as the subscript for B, C$, D and E. That first value is 3; therefore, the third values in lists B, C$, D and E will be written into FILE-Y. Similarly, when I is 2, the second value in list S will be used as the subscript for each of the lists, etc. List A is in sequence so the subscript I is used directly to write its values in FILE-Y.

245

Chapter 24

Using files, communications may be established between programs. Consider a single program which is too large for the memory of the time-sharing system.

LARGE PROGRAM

Figure 24-1

You may divide it into two, more manageable, pieces:

SEGMENT 1		SEGMENT 2

Figure 24-2

You include the CHAIN command as the last statement of Segment 1. When Segment 1 has been executed, the system will automatically begin execution of Segment 2.

Segment 1 and Segment 2 are independent programs. If Segment 1 wants to tell Segment 2 about some values it has computed, then it has to store those values in a file specifically established for the purpose. Here's the way to set up a file to be used by both segments:

```
OLD
OLD FILE NAME--CH3072***
READY.
RENAME
NEW FILE NAME--COMMON
READY.
SAVE
READY.
```

File space for output file COMMON has been established. Segment 1 *writes into* the file. Segment 2 *reads from* the file. You have this arrangement:

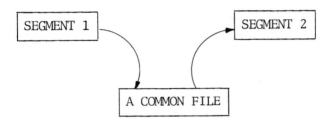

Figure 24-3

Try this next series of programs to see how the technique works. Assume COMMON has been established and saved. The name of the program which follows is LINK1.

```
10   FILES COMMON
20   SCRATCH #1
30   READ A,B,C
40   IF A = 0 THEN 90
50   LET E = A * B * C
60   WRITE #1, A; B; C; E
70   GO TO 30
80   DATA 6,3,4,9,2,6,7,8,8,3,4,7,0,0,0
90   CHAIN LINK2
```

247

Here is LINK2: (This program is written as a separate program and saved after LINK1 has been written and saved.)

```
10 FILES COMMON
20 IF END #1 THEN 60
30 READ #1, X,Y,Z,P
40 PRINT X, Y, Z, P
50 GO TO 20
60 PRINT "END OF ILLUSTRATIVE PROGRAM"
```

To run the program combination, begin with LINK1. Execution of the program will give this result:

LINK1   15:20   03 THU 04/29/71

6	3	4	72
9	2	6	108
7	8	7	392
3	4	7	84

END OF ILLUSTRATIVE PROGRAM

Should you list COMMON, you'll see that it looks like this:

COMMON   15:21   03 THU 04/29/71

1000	6	3	4	72
1010	9	2	6	108
1020	7	8	7	392
1030	3	4	7	84

The following are some miscellaneous techniques for reference:

TO DETERMINE WHETHER AN INTEGER IS ODD OR EVEN

Assume X is the integer (whole number).

```
10   INPUT X
20   LET A = INT(X/2) * 2
30   IF X = A THEN 60
40   PRINT "NUMBER IS ODD";X
50   GO TO 10
60   PRINT "NUMBER IS EVEN";X
70   GO TO 10
```

TO DETERMINE WHETHER AN INTEGER IS EVENLY DIVISIBLE BY A GIVEN INTEGER

Assume X is the dividend and Y is the divisor.

```
10   INPUT X,Y
20   LET Z = INT(X/Y) * Y
30   IF X = Z THEN 60
40   PRINT "NOT EVENLY DIVISIBLE"; X; Y
50   GO TO 10
60   PRINT "EVENLY DIVISIBLE"; X; Y
70   GO TO 10
```

TO COMPUTE THE REMAINDER WHEN AN INTEGER IS DIVIDED BY A GIVEN INTEGER

Assume X is the dividend and Y is the divisor.

```
10   INPUT X,Y
20   LET Z = INT(X/Y) * Y
30   LET R = X - Z
40   PRINT "REMAINDER IS"; R
```

TO FIND A VALUE IN A LIST, WITHIN A RANGE OF VALUES

Assume X is to be found in list A. If a value is within ± .05 of X, a "hit" will be considered to be made:

249

```
    .
    .
    .
80   INPUT X
90   FOR K = 1 TO N
100  IF ABS (X - A(K)) < .05 THEN 140
110  NEXT K
120  PRINT "COULDN'T FIND THE VALUE"; X
130  GO TO 80
140  PRINT "FOUND THE VALUE"; X
150  GO TO 80
```

TO GENERATE A RANDOM INTEGER WITHIN A GIVEN SPAN OF INTEGERS

$$\text{LET } R = \text{INT}(\text{RND}(-1) * N) + B$$

N tells how many different integers are in the series required. B tells which is the beginning integer. For example if the random integer is to be either 11, 12, 13, 14, 15 or 16, the statement is written:

$$\text{LET } R = \text{INT}(\text{RND}(-1) * 6) + 11$$

TO ROUND A VALUE TO A GIVEN NUMBER OF PLACES

Assume X is the value to be rounded:

$$\text{LET } V = \text{INT}(X * P + .5)/P$$

P is a power of 10, such as 10, 100, 1000, etc.

Example: Suppose you wish to round X to 2 decimal places. Use this statement:

$$\text{LET } V = \text{INT}(X * 100 + .5)/100$$

This table tells which P to use for various roundings required:

PLACES	P
0	1
1	10
2	100
3	1000

etc.

TO CONVERT LOG(BASE E) TO LOG(BASE 10)

Multiply log(base e) by .43429448

TO OBTAIN VARIOUS ROOTS

$\sqrt[2]{X} = X^{\frac{1}{2}}$ Ex. LET A = X↑.5

$\sqrt[3]{X} = X^{\frac{1}{3}}$ LET A = X↑.33333333

$\sqrt[4]{X} = X^{\frac{1}{4}}$ LET A = X↑.25

$\sqrt[5]{X} = X^{\frac{1}{5}}$ LET A = X↑.20

etc.

Answers

Chapter 2

1. 10 PRINT 44.8 + 8.63 - .007

2. 10 PRINT 67.43/81.9 + 3.6
   20 PRINT 8.34↑3 + LOG(1.3)

3. 10 PRINT SQR((398.1/4.6)/(14.9/3))

Chapter 3

1. 10 LET X = 1
   20 PRINT SQR(X),X
   30 LET X = X + 1
   40 GO TO 20

2. 10 LET I = .10
   20 PRINT 2500 * I,I
   30 LET I = I + .01
   40 GO TO 20

Chapter 4

1. 10 READ P,N,I,Q
   20 LET A = P * (I + I/Q) ↑ (N * Q)
   30 PRINT P,N,I,Q,A
   40 GO TO 10

(Continued on next page)

```
50 DATA 4163.85,3,.05,4,5000,10,.04,4
60 DATA 1000,14,.05,4,1000,7,.10,12
70 DATA 1000,1,1,10,1000,1,1,100,1000,1,1,1000
```

2.
```
10 READ L,W
20 LET A = L * W
30 PRINT L,W,A
40 GO TO 10
50 DATA 14,65,18.1,47,32,76,13,6,18.3,19.2,11.3
```

Chapter 5

1.
```
10 PRINT "THIS","IS","THE","END"
```

2.
```
10 PRINT "   **********"
```

3.
```
10 PRINT P;Q;R;S;T;U
```

4.
```
10 PRINT "                  COST REPORT YEAR-TO-DATE"
```
Note: There are 25 blanks between " and C in COST.

Chapter 6

1.
```
10 LET N = 11
20 PRINT N,SQR(N),N↑2
30 LET N = N + 1
40 IF N > 20 THEN 60
50 GO TO 20
60 STOP
```

```
2.   10 LET X = 2.71828↑3.14159
     20 LET Y = 3.14159↑2.71828
     30 IF X > Y THEN 60
     40 PRINT "PI TO THE E IS LARGER"
     50 STOP
     60 PRINT "E TO THE PI IS LARGER"
     70 STOP


3.   10 LET A = 1000 * (1 + .06/4)↑(1 * 4)
     20 LET B = 1000 * (1 + .0575/365)↑(1 * 365)
     30 IF A > B THEN 60
     40 PRINT "5 3/4 PERCENT BETTER"
     50 STOP
     60 PRINT "6 PERCENT BETTER"
     70 STOP
```

Chapter 8

```
1.   10 READ A,B,C
     20 IF A = 0 THEN 130
     30 IF A > B THEN 90
     40 IF B > C THEN 70
     50 PRINT "THE LARGEST VALUE IS";C
     60 GO TO 10
     70 PRINT "THE LARGEST VALUE IS";B
     80 GO TO 10
     90 IF A > C THEN 110
    100 GO TO 50
    110 PRINT "THE LARGEST VALUE IS";A
    120 GO TO 10
    130 STOP
    140 DATA 1,2,3,4,4,5,6,6,6,0,0,0
```

2. 10 READ A,B,C

    20 IF A = 0 THEN 80

    30 IF A↑2 + B↑2 = C↑2 THEN 60

    40 PRINT "NOT RIGHT"

    50 GO TO 10

    60 PRINT "RIGHT"

    70 GO TO 10

    80 STOP

    90 DATA 3,4,5,1,2,3,12,5,13,4,7,11,0,0,0

3. 10 LET Z = 0

    20 LET K = 1

    30 READ X

    40 IF X = 1 THEN 60

    50 LET Z = Z + 1

    60 LET K = K + 1

    70 IF K > 20 THEN 90

    80 GO TO 30

    90 PRINT "ZEROES=";Z;"ONES=";20-Z

   100 DATA 0,0,1,1,1,0,1,0,0,1,1,0,0,0,1,1,0,0,1,0

4. 10 LET A = 0

    20 LET B = 0

    30 LET C = 0

    40 LET D = 0

    50 READ X

    60 IF X = 0 THEN 180

    70 IF X < 1 THEN 120

    80 IF X < 2 THEN 140

    90 IF X < 3 THEN 160

   100 LET D = D + 1

(Continued on next page)

```
110 GO TO 50
120 LET A = A + 1
130 GO TO 50
140 LET B = B + 1
150 GO TO 50
160 LET C = C + 1
170 GO TO 50
180 PRINT "VALUES IN FOUR GROUPS ARE";A;B;C;D
190 STOP
200 DATA 3,  6,  2,  1.5,  .5,  3.1,  8.6,  .2
210 DATA 7.4,  1.8,  2.3,  3.4,  4.8,  0
```

5.
```
10 LET S = 0
20 LET K = 1
30 READ N
40 READ X
50 LET S = S + X
60 LET K = K + 1
70 IF K > N THEN 90
80 GO TO 40
90 PRINT S
1000 DATA 10,8,4,7,2,9,4,6,8,9,6
```

Chapter 9

1.
```
10 LET K = 10
20 READ A,B,C,D,E,F,G,H,I,J
30 LET S = A + B + C + D + E + F + G + H + I + J
40 LET V = S/10
50 PRINT V
60 LET S = S - A
70 LET A = B
```

(Continued on next page)

```
80 LET B = C                            (Chapter 9 Cont.)
90 LET C = D
100 LET D = E
110 LET E = F
120 LET F = G
130 LET G = H
140 LET H = I
150 LET I = J
160 LET K = K + 1
170 IF K > 25 THEN 210
180 READ J
190 LET S = S + J
200 GO TO 40
210 STOP
220 DATA 1,2,3,4,5,6,7,8,9,10
230 DATA 11,12,13,14,15,16,17
240 DATA 18,19,20,21,22,23,24,25
```

2.
```
10 LET I = 20
20 LET X1 = -10
30 LET X2 = 10
40 IF ABS(X1 - X2) < .0001 THEN 240
50 LET Y1 = 5 * X1 + 6
60 LET Y2 = 5 * X2 + 6
70 IF Y1 < 0 THEN 90
80 GO TO 140
90 IF Y2 >= 0 THEN 110
100 GO TO 220
110 LET I = I/2
120 LET X1 = X1 + I
130 GO TO 40
```

(Continued on next page)

```
140 IF Y2 < 0 THEN 110
150 IF Y1 < Y2 THEN 190
160 LET X1 = X1 + I
170 LET X2 = X2 + I
180 GO TO 40
190 LET X1 = X1 - I
200 LET X2 = X2 - I
210 GO TO 40
220 IF Y1 < Y2 THEN 160
230 GO TO 190
240 PRINT X1,X2
```

3.
```
10 LET I = 2
20 LET G1 = 10
30 LET G2 = 12
40 LET X1 = 1000*(1+.06/4)↑(G1*4)
50 LET X2 = 1000*(1+.06/4)↑(G2*4)
60 IF X1<10000 THEN 100
70 LET G1 = G1 - I
80 LET G2 = G2 - I
90 GO TO 40
100 IF X2 >= 10000 THEN 140
110 LET G1 = G1 + I
120 LET G2 = G2 + I
130 GO TO 40
140 IF ABS(X1 - X2) < 1 THEN 180
150 LET I = I/2
160 LET G1 = G1 + I
170 GO TO 40
180 PRINT G1, G2
```

Chapter 10

1.　10 INPUT N
　　20 LET W = (8-3)/N
　　30 LET X = W/2
　　40 LET T = 0
　　50 LET K = 1
　　60 LET A = X↑3 * W
　　70 LET T = T + A
　　80 LET X = X + W
　　90 LET K = K + 1
　　100 IF K > N THEN 120
　　110 GO TO 60
　　120 PRINT T
　　130 GO TO 10

2.　10 INPUT N
　　20 LET W = (10-2)/N
　　30 LET X = 2 + W/2
　　40 LET T = 0
　　50 LET K = 1
　　60 LET A = LOG(X) * W
　　70 LET T =T + A
　　80 LET X = X + W
　　90 LET K = K + 1
　　100 IF K > N THEN 120
　　110 GO TO 60
　　120 PRINT T
　　130 GO TO 10

3.　10 INPUT N
　　20 LET W = (5-1)/N

(Continued on next page)

```
30 LET X + 1 + W/2
40 LET T = 0
50 LET K = 1
60 LET A = (3*X+2) * W
70 LET T = T + A
80 LET X = X + W
90 LET K = K + 1
100 IF K > N THEN 120
110 GO TO 60
120 PRINT T
130 GO TO 10
```

Chapter 11

```
1.  10 DIM A(20)
    20 FOR K = 1 TO 20
    30 READ A(K)
    40 NEXT K
    50 FOR K = 1 TO 20
    60 PRINT A(K)
    70 NEXT K
    80 STOP
    90 DATA 3,6,4,7,3,1,4,8,2,4,3,9
    100 DATA 7,4,7,4,3,4,6,4
```

```
2.  10 FOR K = 1 TO 20
    20 READ X
    30 PRINT X
    40 NEXT K
    50 STOP
    60 DATA 3,6,4,7,3,1,4,8,2,4,3,9
    70 DATA 7,4,7,4,3,4,6,4
```

3.  ```
    10 DIM P(10),Q(10)
    20 FOR K = 1 TO 10
    30 READ P(K)
    40 NEXT K
    50 FOR W = 1 TO 10
    60 LET Q(W) = P(W)
    70 NEXT W
    80 FOR L = 1 TO 10
    90 PRINT P(L),Q(L)
    100 NEXT L
    110 STOP
    120 DATA 8,4,7,3,7,9,2,4,1,8
    ```

4.  ```
    10 DIM P(10),Q(10)
    20 FOR K = 1 TO 10
    30 READ P(K)
    40 NEXT K
    50 FOR L = 1 TO 10
    60 LET Q(L) = P(11-L)
    70 NEXT L
    80 FOR N = 1 TO 10
    90 PRINT P(N),Q(N)
    100 NEXT N
    110 STOP
    120 DATA 4,7,3,8,4,2,3,7,4,7
    ```

5.  ```
    10 DIM Q(10)
    20 FOR K = 1 TO 10
    30 READ Q(11 - K)
    40 NEXT K
    50 FOR L = 1 TO 10
    ```

(Continued on next page)

262
    ```

```
      60  PRINT Q(L)                      (Chapter 11 Cont.)
      70  NEXT L
      80  STOP
      90  DATA  4,7,3,8,4,2,3,7,4,7


 6.   10  DIM A(20),B(20)
      20  LET L = 1
      30  READ A(L)
      40  LET L = L + 1
      41  IF L > 20 THEN 50
      42  GO TO 30
      50  LET I = 1
      60  LET S = A(1)
      70  LET W = 1
      80  LET J = 2
      90  IF S < A(J) THEN 120
      100 LET S = A(J)
      110 LET W = J
      120 LET J = J + 1
      121 IF J > 20 THEN 130
      122 GO TO 90
      130 LET B(I) = S
      140 LET A(W) = 9999
      150 LET I = I + 1
      151 IF I > 20 THEN 160
      152 GO TO 60
      160 LET K = 1
      170 PRINT B(K)
      180 LET K = K + 1
      181 IF K > 20 THEN 185
      182 GO TO 170
```

(Continued on next page)

263

185 STOP
190 DATA 7, -9, 8, 9, 7, -3, 10, 5, 11, 6, 9, -6, 4
200 DATA 8, 15, 0, 13, 7, 12, 1

Chapter 12

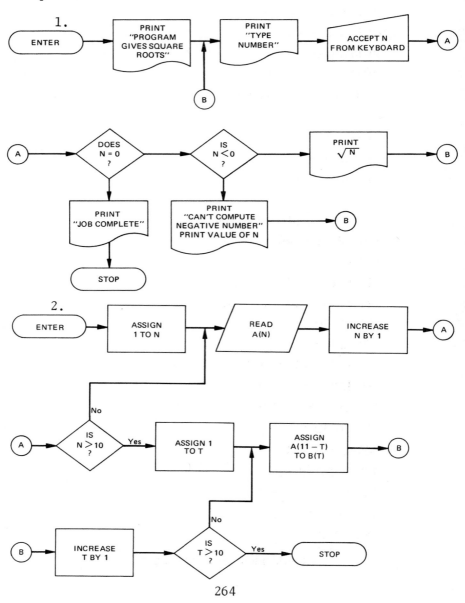

3.

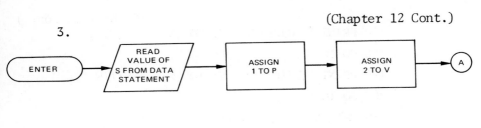

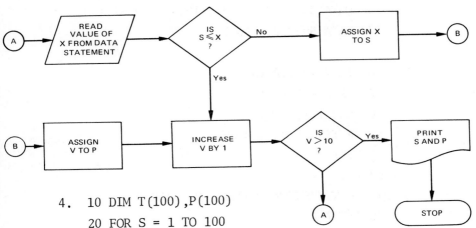

4. 10 DIM T(100),P(100)
    20 FOR S = 1 TO 100
    30 READ T(S),P(S)
    40 IF T(S) = 0 THEN 60
    50 NEXT S
    60 LET S = S - 1
    70 PRINT "ENTER TEMPERATURE VALUE"
    80 INPUT X
    90 FOR W = 1 TO S
    100 IF T(W) > X THEN 140
    110 NEXT W
    120 PRINT "TEMPERATURE NOT IN LIST"
    130 GO TO 70
    140 LET D1 = X - T(W-1)
    150 LET D2 = T(W) - X
    160 IF D1 < D2 THEN 190

(Continued on next page)

```
170 PRINT "VALUE CLOSEST TO";X;" IS";T(W)
180 GO TO 70
190 PRINT "VALUE CLOSEST TO";X;" IS";T(W-1)
200 GO TO 70
210 DATA 8,6,10,8,15,11,20,14,30,18,45
220 DATA 22,80,26,95,30,110,40,150,52,190
230 DATA 59,212,65,0,0
```

5.
```
10 DIM T(100),P(100)
20 FOR S = 1 TO 100
30 READ T(S),P(S)
40 IF T(S) = 0 THEN 60
50 NEXT S
60 LET S = S - 1
70 PRINT "ENTER TEMPERATURE VALUE"
80 INPUT X
90 FOR W = 1 TO S
100 IF T(W) = X THEN 150
110 IF T(W) > X THEN 170
120 NEXT W
130 PRINT "TEMPERATURE NOT IN LIST"
140 GO TO 70
150 PRINT T(W),P(W)
160 GO TO 70
170 LET D1 = X - T(W-1)
180 LET D2 = T(W) - T(W-1)
190 LET D3 = P(W) - P(W-1)
200 LET A = (D1*D3)/D2
210 PRINT S,P(W-1) + A
220 GO TO 70
230 DATA 8,6,10,8,15,11,20,14,30,18,45
```

(Continued on next page)

```
240 DATA 22,80,26,95,30,110,40,150,52,190
250 DATA 59,212,65,0,0
```

6.
```
10 DIM A(20)
20 LET S = 0
30 FOR K = 1 TO 20
40 READ A(K)
50 LET S = S + A(K)
60 NEXT K
70 LET V = S/20
80 LET P = 0
90 FOR L = 1 TO 20
100 LET P = P + (V-A(L))↑2
110 NEXT L
120 LET D = SQR(P/19)
130 PRINT V,D
140 STOP
150 DATA 8,3,4,7,6,7,4,1,9,4,3,2
160 DATA 7,9,3,7,1,2,4,6
```

7.
```
10 DIM A(20)
20 FOR K = 1 TO 20
30 READ A(K)
40 NEXT K
50 FOR J = 1 TO 20
60 LET C = (A(J) - 32) * (5/9)
70 PRINT A(J),C
80 NEXT J
90 STOP
100 DATA 40,50,35,32,0,10,-10,15,75,45
110 DATA 100,212,-20,80,90,20,30,70,72,120
```

8.  ```
    10 DIM A(20),B(20),C(20)
    20 FOR M = 1 TO 20
    30 LET B(M) = 0
    40 LET C(M) = 0
    50 NEXT M
    60 FOR N = 1 TO 20
    70 READ A(N)
    80 NEXT N
    90 LET L = 0
    100 LET M = 0
    110 FOR K = 1 TO 20
    120 LET X = INT(A(K)/2) * 2
    130 IF X = A(K) THEN 170
    140 LET L = L + 1
    150 LET B(L) = A(K)
    160 GO TO 190
    170 LET M = M + 1
    180 LET C(M) = A(K)
    190 NEXT K
    200 FOR L = 1 TO 20
    210 PRINT A(L),B(L),C(L)
    220 NEXT L
    230 DATA 3,5,21,12,6,7,4,50,75,69
    240 DATA 4,20,15,26,28,33,60,68,80,90
    ```

9.  ```
    10 DIM A(20)
    20 FOR L = 1 TO 20
    30 READ A(L)
    40 NEXT L
    50 LET X = 0
    60 LET Y = 0
    ```

(Continued on next page)

```
70 LET Z = 0
80 FOR K = 1 TO 20
90 IF A(K) < 10 THEN 130
100 IF A(K) < 20 THEN 150
110 LET Z = Z + 1
120 GO TO 160
130 LET X = X + 1
140 GO TO 160
150 LET Y = Y + 1
160 NEXT K
170 PRINT "VALUES IN 3 CATEGORIES ARE";X;Y;Z
180 STOP
190 DATA 11,3,23,13,24,4,12,35,5,1
200 DATA 21,14,6,22,15,7,30,40,33,16
```

10.
```
10 DIM A(20),B(10),C(10)
11 FOR W = 1 TO 20
12 LET A(W) = 0
13 NEXT W
20 FOR N = 1 TO 10
30 READ B(N),C(N)
40 NEXT N
50 LET L = 1
60 LET M = 1
70 LET K = 1
80 LET X = B(L)
90 LET Y = C(M)
100 IF X < Y THEN 200
110 LET A(K) = Y
120 LET K = K + 1
130 IF K > 20 THEN 190
```

(Continued on next page)

```
140 LET M = M + 1
150 IF M > 10 THEN 170
160 GO TO 90
170 LET Y = 9999
180 GO TO 100
190 FOR P = 1 TO 10
191 PRINT A(P),B(P),C(P)
192 NEXT P
193 FOR P = 11 TO 20
194 PRINT A(P)
195 NEXT P
196 STOP
200 LET A(K) = X
210 LET K = K + 1
220 K > 20 THEN 190
230 LET L = L + 1
240 IF L > 10 THEN 270
250 LET X = B(L)
260 GO TO 100
270 LET X = 9999
280 GO TO 100
290 DATA 11,14,23,45,47,56,65,70,71,75
300 DATA 77,81,85,89,91,93,99,101,103,109
```

Chapter 14

```
1.  10 LET A = 0
    20 LET B = 0
    30 LET C = 0
    40 LET D = 0
    50 LET E = 0
    60 LET F = 0
```

(Continued on next page)

```
70 LET G = 0
80 LET H = 0
90 LET I = 0
100 LET J = 0
120 FOR W = 1 TO 1000
130 LET R = RND(-1)
140 IF R<.1 THEN 250
150 IF R<.2 THEN 270
160 IF R<.3 THEN 290
170 IF R<.4 THEN 310
180 IF R<.5 THEN 330
190 IF R<.6 THEN 350
200 IF R<.7 THEN 370
210 IF R<.8 THEN 390
220 IF R<.9 THEN 410
230 LET J = J + 1
240 GO TO 420
250 LET A = A + 1
260 GO TO 420
270 LET B = B + 1
280 GO TO 420
290 LET C = C + 1
300 GO TO 420
310 LET D = D + 1
320 GO TO 420
330 LET E = E + 1
340 GO TO 420
350 LET F = F + 1
360 GO TO 420
370 LET G = G + 1
380 GO TO 420
```

(Continued on next page)

```
390 LET H = H + 1
400 GO TO 420
410 LET I = I + 1
420 NEXT W
430 PRINT A,B,C,D,E,F,G,H,I,J
440 STOP
```

2.
```
10 LET S = 0
20 FOR K = 1 TO 1000
30 LET R = RND(-1)
40 LET S = S + R
50 NEXT K
60 PRINT S/1000
70 STOP
```

3.
```
10 LET T = 0
20 FOR K = 1 TO 20
30 LET D = 20
40 LET N = 0
50 LET N = N + 1
60 LET X = RND(-1)
70 IF X < .5 THEN 110
80 LET D = D + 1
90 IF D = 40 THEN 140
100 GO TO 50
110 LET D = D - 1
120 IF D = 0 THEN 160
130 GO TO 50
140 PRINT "RIGHT, ";N;"STEPS"
150 GO TO 170
160 PRINT " LEFT, ";N;"STEPS"
```

(Continued on next page)

272

```
170 LET T = T + N
180 NEXT K
190 LET V = T/20
200 PRINT "AVERAGE IS";V
210 STOP
```

4.
```
10 LET T = 0
20 FOR K = 1 TO 100
30 LET S = 0
40 LET R = RND(-1)
50 LET T = T + 1
60 LET S = S + R
70 IF S > 1 THEN 90
80 GO TO 40
90 NEXT K
100 PRINT "AVERAGE IS";T/100
```

5.
```
10 LET T = 0
20 FOR K = 1 TO 20
30 LET D = 20
40 LET N = 0
50 LET N = N + 1
60 LET X = RND(-1)
70 IF X < .5 THEN 110
80 LET D = D + 1
90 IF D = 40 THEN 140
100 GO TO 50
110 LET D = D - 1
120 IF D = 0 THEN 160
130 GO TO 50
140 PRINT " PAT WINS, ";N;"TOSSES"
```

(Continued on next page)

```
150 GO TO 170
160 PRINT 'MIKE WINS, '';N;''TOSSES''
170 LET T = T + N
180 NEXT K
190 LET V = T/20
200 PRINT ''AVERAGE IS'';V
210 STOP
```

6.

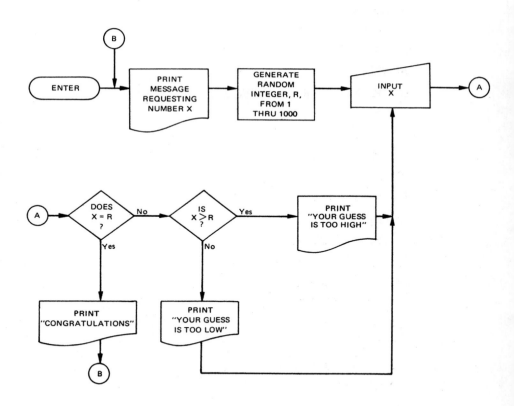

Chapter 15

1. 10 LET R = IND(RND(-1)*11) + 5

2. 10 LET X = 0
    20 LET Y = 0
    30 FOR K = 1 TO 500
    40 LET X1 = X
    50 LET Y1 = Y
    60 LET R = INT(RND(-1)*4) + 1
    70 ON R GO TO 100,200,300,400
    100 LET X = X + 1
    110 GO TO 500
    200 LET X = X - 1
    210 GO TO 500
    300 LET Y = Y + 1
    310 GO TO 500
    400 LET Y = Y - 1
    500 IF X <- 20 THEN 600
    510 IF X > 20 THEN 600
    520 IF Y <- 20 THEN 600
    530 IF Y > 20 THEN 600
    540 GO TO 700
    600 LET X = X1
    610 LET Y = Y1
    620 GO TO 60
    700 NEXT K
    710 PRINT X, Y

3. 10 LET X1 = 8
    20 LET Y1 = 1
    30 LET X2 = 1

(Continued on next page)

```
40 LET Y2 = 8
50 LET K = 0
60 LET S1 = X1
70 LET T1 = Y1
80 LET S2 = X2
90 LET T2 = Y2
100 LET R = INT(RND(-1)*8) + 1
110 ON R GO TO 120,150,180,210,240,270,300,330
120 LET X1 = X1 + 2
130 LET Y1 = Y1 + 1
140 GO TO 360
150 LET X1 = X1 + 2
160 LET Y1 = Y1 - 1
170 GO TO 360
180 LET X1 = X1 - 2
190 LET Y1 = Y1 + 1
200 GO TO 360
210 LET X1 = X1 - 2
220 LET Y1 = Y1 - 1
230 GO TO 360
240 LET X1 = X1 + 1
250 LET Y1 = Y1 + 2
260 GO TO 360
270 LET X1 = X1 + 1
280 LET Y1 = Y1 - 2
290 GO TO 360
300 LET X1 = X1 - 1
310 LET Y1 = Y1 + 2
320 GO TO 360
330 LET X1 = X1 - 1
340 LET Y1 = Y1 - 2
350 GO TO 360
```

(Continued on next page)

```
360   IF X1 > 8 THEN 780                    (Chapter 15 Cont.)
370   IF X1 < 1 THEN 780
380   IF Y1 > 8 THEN 780
390   IF Y1 < 1 THEN 780
400   LET R = INT(RND(-1)*8) + 1
410   ON R GO TO 420,450,480,510,540,570,600,630
420   LET X2 = X2 + 2
430   LET Y2 = Y2 + 1
440   GO TO 660
450   LET X2 = X2 + 2
460   LET Y2 = Y2 - 1
470   GO TO 660
480   LET X2 = X2 - 2
490   LET Y2 = Y2 + 1
500   GO TO 660
510   LET X2 = X2 - 2
520   LET Y2 = Y2 - 1
530   GO TO 660
540   LET X2 = X2 + 1
550   LET Y2 = Y2 + 2
560   GO TO 660
570   LET X2 = X2 + 1
580   LET Y2 = Y2 - 2
590   GO TO 660
600   LET X2 = X2 - 1
610   LET Y2 = Y2 + 2
620   GO TO 660
630   LET X2 = X2 - 1
640   LET Y2 = Y2 - 2
650   GO TO 660
660   IF X2 > 8 THEN 810
670   IF X2 < 1 THEN 810
```
(Continued on next page)

```
680   IF Y2 > 8 THEN 810
690   IF Y2 < 1 THEN 810
700   LET K = K + 1
710   IF X1 = X2 THEN 730
720   GO TO 60
730   IF Y1 = Y2 THEN 750
740   GO TO 60
750   PRINT "KNIGHTS COLLIDE AT X=";X1;",   Y=";Y1
760   PRINT "NUMBER OF JUMPS=";K
770   STOP
780   LET X1 = S1
790   LET Y1 = T1
800   GO TO 100
810   LET X2 = S2
820   LET Y2 = T2
830   GO TO 400
```

Chapter 16

```
1.   10   LET S = 0
     20   FOR K = 1 TO 100
     30   FOR L = 1 TO 100
     40   LET R = INT(RND(-1)*100) + 1
     50   IF R = 1 THEN 70
     60   GO TO 90
     70   LET S = S + 1
     80   GO TO 100
     90   NEXT L
     100   NEXT K
     110   PRINT S/100
     120   GO TO 10
```

2.
```
10   DIM D(366)
20   FOR K = 1 TO 366
30   LET D(K) = 0
40   NEXT K
50   FOR K = 1 TO 23
60   LET R = INT(RND(-1)*366) + 1
70   LET D(R) = D(R) + 1
80   NEXT K
90   FOR K = 1 TO 366
100  IF D(K) > 1 THEN 140
110  NEXT K
120  PRINT "TWO BIRTHDAYS NOT SAME"
130  GO TO 20
140  PRINT "TWO BIRTHDAYS ARE SAME"
150  GO TO 20
```

3.
```
10   DIM T(100)
20   PRINT "DAY","NUM OUT","GOT BACK","SENT OUT"
30   PRINT
40   FOR I = 1 TO 79
50   LET T(I) = 1
60   NEXT I
70   FOR I = 80 TO 100
80   LET T(I) = 0
90   NEXT I
100  FOR I = 1 TO 79
110  LET J = T(I)
120  PRINT I,I,J-1,J
130  FOR K = 1 TO J
140  LET R = INT(RND(-1)*17) + 5
150  LET T(I+R) = T(I+R) + 1
```

(Continued on next page)

```
160   NEXT K
170   NEXT I
180   LET Z = 79
190   FOR I = 80 TO 100
200   LET Z = Z - T(I)
210   PRINT I,Z,T(I),0
220   NEXT I
230   STOP
```

```
4.    10   DIM A(41)
      20   PRINT "POCKET","CONTENTS","HISTOGRAM"
      30   PRINT
      40   FOR L = 1 TO 41
      50   LET A(L) = 0
      60   NEXT L
      70   FOR K = 1 TO 1000
      80   LET P = 21
      90   FOR M = 1 TO 40
      100  LET X = RND(-1)
      110  IF X > .5 THEN 140
      120  LET P = P - .5
      130  GO TO 150
      140  LET P = P + .5
      150  NEXT M
      160  LET A(P) = A(P) + 1
      170  NEXT K
      180  FOR W = 1 TO 41
      190  PRINT W,A(W),
      200  IF A(W) = 0 THEN 420
      210  IF A(W) < 10 THEN 440
      220  IF A(W) < 20 THEN 460
```

(Continued on next page)

```
230   IF A(W) < 30 THEN 480
240   IF A(W) < 40 THEN 500
250   IF A(W) < 50 THEN 520
260   IF A(W) < 60 THEN 540
270   IF A(W) < 70 THEN 560
280   IF A(W) < 80 THEN 580
290   IF A(W) < 90 THEN 600
300   IF A(W) < 100 THEN 620
310   IF A(W) < 110 THEN 640
320   IF A(W) < 120 THEN 660
330   IF A(W) < 130 THEN 680
340   IF A(W) < 140 THEN 700
350   IF A(W) < 150 THEN 720
360   IF A(W) < 160 THEN 740
370   IF A(W) < 170 THEN 760
380   IF A(W) < 180 THEN 780
390   IF A(W) < 190 THEN 800
400   PRINT "********************"
410   GO TO 820
420   PRINT
430   GO TO 820
440   PRINT "*"
450   GO TO 820
460   PRINT "**"
470   GO TO 820
480   PRINT "***"
490   GO TO 820
500   PRINT "****"
510   GO TO 820
520   PRINT "*****"
530   GO TO 820
```

(Continued on next page)

```
540   PRINT "******"
550   GO TO 820
560   PRINT "*******"
570   GO TO 820
580   PRINT "********"
590   GO TO 820
600   PRINT "*********"
610   GO TO 820
620   PRINT "**********"
630   GO TO 820
640   PRINT "***********"
650   GO TO 820
660   PRINT "************"
670   GO TO 820
680   PRINT "*************"
690   GO TO 820
700   PRINT "**************"
710   GO TO 820
720   PRINT "***************"
730   GO TO 820
740   PRINT "****************"
750   GO TO 820
760   PRINT "*****************"
770   GO TO 820
780   PRINT "******************"
790   GO TO 820
800   PRINT "*******************"
810   GO TO 820
820   NEXT W
830   STOP
```

Chapter 17

1.　10　DIM A(11),B(11)
　　20　FOR W = 1 TO 11
　　30　READ A(W)
　　40　NEXT W
　　50　FOR I = 1 TO 11
　　60　LET S = A(1)
　　70　LET P = 1
　　80　FOR J = 2 TO 11
　　90　IF A(J) < S THEN 110
　　100　GO TO 130
　　110　LET S = A(J)
　　120　LET P = J
　　130　NEXT J
　　140　LET B(I) = S
　　150　LET A(P) = 99999
　　160　NEXT I
　　170　FOR Y = 1 TO 11
　　180　PRINT B(Y)
　　190　NEXT Y
　　200　STOP
　　210　DATA 10,6,8,3,12,15,3,1,7,11,8

2.　10　DIM A(11)
　　20　FOR S = 1 TO 11
　　30　READ A(S)
　　40　NEXT S
　　50　FOR N = 10 TO 1 STEP -1
　　60　LET F = 0
　　70　FOR J = 1 TO N
　　80　IF A(J) < A(J+1) THEN 130

(Continued on next page)

```
90   LET T = A(J)
100  LET A(J) = A(J+1)
110  LET A(J+1) = T
120  LET F = 1
130  NEXT J
140  IF F = 0 THEN 160
150  NEXT N
160  FOR X = 1 TO 11
170  PRINT A(X)
180  NEXT X
190  STOP
200  DATA 10,6,8,3,12,15,3,1,7,11,8
```

3.
```
10   DIM A(11)
20   FOR K = 1 TO 11
30   READ A(K)
40   NEXT K
50   LET D = 1
60   LET D = D * 2
70   LET J = INT(11/D)
80   IF J = 0 THEN 270
90   LET L = 1
100  LET H = I + J
110  IF H > 11 THEN 60
120  LET L1 = L
130  LET H1 = H
140  IF A(H) > A(L) THEN 220
150  LET T = A(L)
160  LET A(L) = A(H)
170  LET A(H) = T
180  LET L = L - J
```

(Continued on next page)

284

```
190   IF L < 1 THEN 220
200   LET H = H - J
210   GO TO 140
220   LET L = L1
230   LET H = H1
240   LET L = L + 1
250   LET H = H + 1
260   GO TO 110
270   FOR K = 1 TO 11
280   PRINT A(K)
290   NEXT K
300   DATA 10,6,8,3,12,15,3,1,7,11,8
```

Chapter 18

```
1.    10   DIM A(20),B(10),C(10)
      20   FOR I = 1 TO 20
      30   READ A(I)
      40   PRINT A(I);
      50   NEXT I
      60   PRINT
      70   LET J = 1
      80   FOR I = 1 TO 10
      90   LET B(I) = A(J)
      100  LET J = J + 1
      110  LET C(I) = A(J)
      120  LET J = J + 1
      130  NEXT I
      140  LET J = 1
      150  LET K = 1
      160  FOR I = 1 TO 20
      170  IF B(J) < C(K) THEN 220
```

(Continued on next page)

```
180   LET A(I) = C(K)
190   LET K = K + 1
200   IF K > 10 THEN 270
210   GO TO 260
220   LET A(I) = B(J)
230   LET J = J + 1
240   IF J > 10 THEN 340
250   GO TO 260
260   NEXT I
270   LET I = I + 1
280   FOR N = I TO 20
290   LET A(I) = B(J)
300   LET I = I + 1
310   LET J = J + 1
320   NEXT N
330   GO TO 400
340   LET I = I + 1
350   FOR N = I TO 20
360   LET A(I) = C(K)
370   LET I = I + 1
380   LET K = K + 1
390   NEXT N
400   FOR I = 1 TO 20
410   PRINT A(I);
420   NEXT I
430   PRINT
440   FOR I = 1 TO 19
450   IF A(I) < = A(I+1) THEN 470
460   GO TO 70
470   NEXT I
480   PRINT "JOB COMPLETE"
```

(Continued on next page)

```
490   STOP
500   DATA 13,16,12,18,6,8,112,7,6,3,19,11,5,4,1,15,4,
510   DATA 11,9,5
```

Chapter 19

1.
```
10    INPUT A$
20    IF A$ = "ZERO" THEN 200
30    IF A$ = "ONE" THEN 300
40    IF A$ = "TWO" THEN 400
50    IF A$ = "THREE" THEN 500
60    IF A$ = "FOUR" THEN 600
70    IF A$ = "FIVE" THEN 700
80    IF A$ = "SIX" THEN 800
90    IF A$ = "SEVEN" THEN 900
100   IF A$ = "EIGHT" THEN 1000
110   IF A$ = "NINE" THEN 1100
120   IF A$ = "FINIS" THEN 1200
130   PRINT "DIGIT NOT FOUND"
140   GO TO 10
200   PRINT 0
210   GO TO 10
300   PRINT 1
310   GO TO 10
400   PRINT 2
410   GO TO 10
500   PRINT 3
510   GO TO 10
600   PRINT 4
610   GO TO 10
700   PRINT 5
710   GO TO 10
```

(Continued on next page)

```
800   PRINT 6
810   GO TO 10
900   PRINT 7
910   GO TO 10
1000  PRINT 8
1010  GO TO 10
1100  PRINT 9
1110  GO TO 10
1200  STOP
```

2.
```
10   INPUT A$,X,Y
20   IF A$ = "ADD" THEN 100
30   IF A$ = "SUBTRACT" THEN 200
40   IF A$ = "MULTIPLY" THEN 300
50   IF A$ = "DIVIDE" THEN 400
60   IF A$ = "DONE" THEN 500
70   PRINT "OPERATION NOT FOUND"
80   GO TO 10
100  PRINT X + Y
110  GO TO 10
200  PRINT X - Y
210  GO TO 10
300  PRINT X * Y
310  GO TO 10
400  PRINT X / Y
410  GO TO 10
500  STOP
```

3.
```
10   DIM O$(100),O(100),V(100)
20   FOR I = 1 TO 100
30   READ O$(I),O(I),T$
```

(Continued on next page)

```
40   IF O$(I) = "END" THEN 55
50   NEXT I
55   LET C = 0
60   LET C = C + 1
70   LET Q$ = O$(C)
80   IF Q$ = "DEF" THEN 300
90   IF Q$ = "ADD" THEN 400
100  IF Q$ = "SUB" THEN 500
110  IF Q$ = "MPY" THEN 600
120  IF Q$ = "DIV" THEN 700
130  IF Q$ = "TPL" THEN 800
140  IF Q$ = "TMI" THEN 900
150  IF Q$ = "TZE" THEN 1000
160  IF Q$ = "TRU" THEN 1100
170  IF Q$ = "CLA" THEN 1200
180  IF Q$ = "STA" THEN 1300
190  IF Q$ = "SIN" THEN 1400
200  IF Q$ = "SQR" THEN 1500
210  IF Q$ = "LOG" THEN 1600
220  IF Q$ = "COS" THEN 1700
230  IF Q$ = "CMP" THEN 1800
240  IF Q$ = "PRT" THEN 1900
245  IF Q$ = "PRL" THEN 1950
250  IF Q$ = "STP" THEN 2000
260  PRINT "COULDN'T FIND OP"
270  STOP
300  LET V(C) = O(C)
310  GO TO 60
400  LET A = A + V(O(C))
410  GO TO 60
500  LET A = A - V(O(C))
```

This program interprets the data found beginning with line 5000 as an executable program in assembly language.

The operations which the assembly language understands, are shown on page 192 and in this listing (lines 80 through 250).

In assembly programs, locations are numbered 1,2,3, etc., and correspond with line numbers 5010, 5020, 5030, etc. Thus, at line 5070, the instruction says: "load into the accumulator the contents of location 4." Location 4 corresponds to line 5040, which contains a value of R. The value was read into location 4 at line 5060.

(Continued on next page)

```
510   GO TO 60
600   LET A = A * V(O(C))
610   GO TO 60
700   LET A = A/V(O(C))
710   GO TO 60
800   IF I > 0 THEN 820
810   GO TO 60
820   LET C = O(C)
830   GO TO 70
900   IF I < 1 THEN 920
910   GO TO 60
920   LET C = O(C)
930   GO TO 70
1000   IF I = 0 THEN 1020
1010   GO TO 60
1020   LET C = O(C)
1030   GO TO 70
1100   LET C = O(C)
1110   GO TO 70
1200   LET A = V(O(C))
1210   GO TO 60
1300   LET V(O(C)) = A
1310   GO TO 60
1400   LET A = SIN(A)
1410   GO TO 60
1500   LET A = SQR(A)
1510   GO TO 60
1600   LET A = LOG(A)
1610   GO TO 60
1700   LET A = COS(A)
1710   GO TO 60
```

The program shown on page 191 and 192 computes circumferences of circles using radius values 1,2,3,4 and 5.

(Continued on next page)

```
1800   LET I = A
1810   LET I = I - V(O(C))
1820   GO TO 60
1900   PRINT V(O(C)),
1910   GO TO 60
1950   PRINT V(O(C))
1960   GO TO 60
2000   STOP
```

Chapter 20

1.
```
10   PRINT "              -2              -1              0";
20   PRINT "               1               2"
30   LET X = .1
40   LET V = LOG(X)
50   IF V < 0 THEN 90
60   LET P = INT(36+12*V)
70   PRINT X; TAB(36);"*";TAB(P);"X"
80   GO TO 110
90   LET P = INT((3-ABS(V))*12)
100  PRINT X;TAB(P);"X";TAB(36);"*"
110  LET X = X + .1
120  IF ABS(1 - X) < .001 THEN 150
130  IF X > 5 THEN 170
140  GO TO 40
150  PRINT X;TAB(36);"X"
160  GO TO 110
170  PRINT "              -2              -1              0";
180  PRINT "               1               2"
```

2.
```
10   PRINT "           2    4    6    8    10   12   14";
20   PRINT "  16    18    20    22   24"
```

(Continued on next page)

```
    30   LET X = -5                              (Chapter 20 Cont.)
    40   LET V = X↑2
    50   LET P = INT(V*2.4) + 6
    60   PRINT X;TAB(P);"X"
    70   LET X = X + .2
    80   IF ABS(X) < .001 THEN 110
    90   IF X > 5 THEN 140
   100   GO TO 40
   110   PRINT 0;"***********************************";
   120   PRINT "******************************"
   130   GO TO 70
   140   PRINT "          2    4    6    8   10   12   14";
   150   PRINT "   16   18   20   22   24"


3. 10   PRINT "   -5    0    5   10   15   20   25   30";
    20   PRINT "   35   40   45   50"
    30   LET X = -3
    40   LET V = 3 * X↑2 - 7 * X + 1
    50   LET P = INT(V) + 10
    60   IF V < 0 THEN 180
    70   PRINT X;TAB(9);"*";TAB(P);"X"
    80   LET X = X + .2
    90   IF ABS(X) < .001 THEN 120
   100   IF X > 5 THEN 150
   110   GO TO 40
   120   PRINT 0;"***********************************";
   130   PRINT "******************************"
   140   GO TO 80
   150   PRINT "   -5    0    5   10   15   20   25   30";
   160   PRINT "   35   40   45   50"
   170   STOP
   180   PRINT X;TAB(P);"X";TAB(9);"*"
   190   GO TO 80
```

292

```
3.    10   FILES FILE-X; FILE-Y
      20   LET N = 0
      30   DIM A(100),B(100),C$(100),D(100),E(100)
      40   DIM S(100)
      50   FOR J = 1 TO 100
      60   LET S(J) = J
      70   NEXT J
      80   FOR I = 1 TO 100
      90   IF END #1 THEN 150
     100   READ #1,A(I),B(I),C$(I),D(I),E(I)
     110   LET N = N + 1
     120   NEXT I
     130   PRINT "TOO MANY RECORDS IN FILE TO SORT"
     140   STOP
     150   LET D = 1
     160   LET D = D * 2
     170   LET J = INT(N/D)
     180   IF J = 0 THEN 400
     190   LET L = 1
     200   LET H = I + J
     210   IF H > N THEN 160
     220   LET L1 = L
     230   LET H1 = H
     240   IF A(H) > A(L) THEN 350
     250   LET T = S(L)
     260   LET S(L) = S(H)
     270   LET S(H) = T
     280   LET T = A(L)
     290   LET A(L) = A(H)
     300   LET A(H) = T
```

(Continued on next page)

```
310   LET L = L - J
320   IF L < 1 THEN 350
330   LET H = H - J
340   GO TO 240
350   LET L = L1
360   LET H = H1
370   LET L = L + 1
380   LET H = H + 1
390   GO TO 210
400   SCRATCH #2
410   FOR I = 1 TO N
420   WRITE #2,A(I);B(S(I));C$(S(I));D(S(I));E(S(I))
430   NEXT I
```

Index

298